TWAYNE'S WORLD AUTHORS SERIES

A Survey of the World's Literature

Sylvia E. Bowman, Indiana University

GENERAL EDITOR

FRANCE

Maxwell A. Smith, Guerry Professor of French, Emeritus
The University of Chattanooga
Former Visiting Professor in Modern Languages
The Florida State University

EDITOR

D0125720

Lamartine

(TWAS 254)

TWAYNE'S WORLD AUTHORS SERIES (TWAS)

The purpose of TWAS is to survey the major writers —novelists, dramatists, historians, poets, philosophers, and critics—of the nations of the world. Among the national literatures covered are those of Australia, Canada, China, Eastern Europe, France, Germany, Greece, India, Italy, Japan, Latin America, the Netherlands, New Zealand, Poland, Russia, Scandinavia, Spain, and the African nations, as well as Hebrew, Yiddish, and Latin Classical literatures. This survey is complemented by Twayne's United States Authors Series and English Authors Series.

The intent of each volume in these series is to present a critical-analytical study of the works of the writer; to include biographical and historical material that may be necessary for understanding, appreciation, and critical appraisal of the writer; and to present all material in clear, concise English—but not to vitiate the scholarly content of the work by doing so.

Lamartine

By CHARLES M. LOMBARD

University of Illinois

Twayne Publishers :: New York

Preface

Lamartine's reputation has suffered somewhat in recent years, the centennial of his death in 1969 being the occasion for scathing remarks about the outmoded sentimentalism of the *Méditations* and *Harmonies*. There is nonetheless a question in the mind of some critics whether he merits the oblivion to which his detractors would gladly assign him.

Although already the subject of considerable study, some questions concerning the evaluation of Lamartine's religious views remain unanswered. In addition, little note is usually taken of his numerous works written after 1840. While much of Lamartine's later production lacks the quality of earlier years, it still deserves the attention of any serious student of Lamartine.

In the study at hand a sketch of Lamartine's life includes a synopsis of the main events in his political career. An attempt is made to present a unified impression of his principal poetic works, the *Méditations* and *Harmonies*, together with a summary and analysis of other writings. The *Cours familier de littérature*, in particular, is outlined volume by volume to serve as a guide to Lamartine's major prose work after 1850. Since the poet was obsessed with the dilemma of man's relationship to the Creator, the steps in his thinking as reflected in his writings are analyzed. There is also an appraisal of Lamartine's concept of the novel and the theater on the basis of his own efforts in these genres. It is hoped that the present study will contribute to a better understanding of a noteworthy figure in French history and letters.

Contents

Preface

Contents

Chronology

Chronology

resignation of Executive Commission to Assembly. December 10, defeated for presidency by Louis-Napoleon.

1849 January 20, *Raphaël* published. April, *Conseiller du peuple* starts publication. Publication of *Les Confidences* and *Graziella* and the *Histoire de la Révolution de 1848*.

1850 Publication of *Geneviève*.

1851 First volumes of the *Histoire de la Restauration* appear. April 6, *Toussaint l'Ouverture* presented at Porte Saint-Martin. December 2, Lamartine quits public life after Louis-Napoleon's coup d'état. Publication of *Le Tailleur de pierres de Saint-Point* and *Nouvelles Confidences*.

1852 Publication of the *Civilisateur*.

1854 Publication of the *Histoire de la Russie*.

1855 The four volumes of the *Histoire des Constituants* appear. Publication of the *Histoire de la Turquie*.

1856 Lamartine starts publication of the *Cours familier de littérature*.

1858 Various attempts by private and public agencies to alleviate Lamartine's financial burden.

1863 Publication of *Mémoires politiques*.

1864 Publication of *La France parlementaire* and *Shakespeare et son œuvre*.

1865 Publication of *Civilisateurs et conquérants*.

1867 Publication of *Antoniella*. Lamartine is stricken with apoplexy and fails rapidly.

1869 February 28, dies in Paris and is buried at Saint-Point.

CHAPTER 1

Life of Lamartine

I Early Years

ALPHONSE-Marie-Louis de Prat de Lamartine was descended from a sturdy line of minor nobility. Born at Mâcon on October 21, 1790, he was the center of attraction as the only son. His mother and five sisters contributed to the development of his at times almost feminine sensibilities. The Chevalier de Lamartine, his father, favored the views of the Enlightenment. Lamartine's mother, Alix des Roys, married the Chevalier on January 7, 1790. During the French Revolution his father was jailed at Vaugirard. According to Lamartine's own melodramatic account, his mother took up residence near the prison, communicated with her husband, and helped him to slip out at night so they could be temporarily reunited.[1]

After the Reign of Terror, the Lamartines returned to the small family estate at Milly. The young Alphonse was a fun-loving urchin who indulged in boyish pranks with village pals. Packed off to the Institut Puppier in 1801, he revolted against the disagreeable conditions there and attempted to run away. Forced to return with a severe reprimand, he eventually had his way and was transferred to Belley, a finishing school conducted by ex-Jesuits known as the Fathers of the Faith.

Life at Belley was more to Lamartine's liking. The priests had a more liberal approach to literature and philosophy than the Puppier faculty. New companions shared Alphonse's growing interest in letters. Together they read the great works of French writers and those of foreign authors like Goethe and Pope. With sentimentalism in fashion, the writings of Chateaubriand were highly topical. The *Genius of Christianity* and *Atala* had created a vogue for an emotional attachment to the impressive externals of Catholic worship. At Belley the future poet experienced the

11

full effects of the current emphasis on liturgical ritual and return
to traditional religion. Previously Lamartine had been prepared
for Belley by his mother. Madame Lamartine, while not a dogmatic Catholic, cherished the spiritual solace provided by the
Church. She had met Rousseau in her youth and valued his
writings almost as much as the Bible and the *Imitation of Christ*.
Thus predisposed to the emotional appeal of Catholicism, Lamartine responded wholeheartedly to the environment at Belley,
where he was remembered as a dreamer and imaginative story-
teller.

II *Adolescence and Early Loves*

The starry-eyed student was also a lusty adolescent fond of
outdoor sports and fencing. By the age of fifteen he probably
had already had several love affairs. Upon graduation from
Belley, he was content to play the gay young blade. Aside from
pretty teen-age girls only literature interested him. A liaison
with the daughter of a local magistrate ended in a trip to Italy
in 1811. The passionate romance with Antoniella, an employee
of a tobacco plant, laid the basis for the novel *Graziella*. Lamartine, always insisting on the treasured recollections of the Italian
idyl, returned to France to meet Nina de Pierreclos by whom he
apparently had a son.

In 1815 the tide of political events caught up with Lamartine.
The family regarded Napoleon as a usurper, and the elder
Lamartine had Alphonse named mayor of Milly in 1812 to avoid
conscription. With Bonaparte's exile to Elba and the return of
Louis XVIII, Lamartine, true to his father's Bourbonist traditions,
enlisted in the Gardes du Corps. During the Hundred Days he
fled to Switzerland and found time for a liaison with Geneviève
Favre. A year after Waterloo the love that was to affect much of
his writing began in October, 1816, at Aix-les-Bains. Julie Charles,
wife of a celebrated physicist, and Alphonse fell desperately in
love. Her death on December 18, 1817, inspired the poem "Le
Crucifix," a sincere reflection of the grief Lamartine felt. *Raphaël*,
published years later, was a romanticized version of their affair.

To forget Julie's death he plunged himself into literary activity.
Saül, a drama modeled on Racinian and Shakespearean lines,

was suggested to the celebrated Talma who declined to appear in the title role. Undaunted, Lamartine continued to write poetry. The *Méditations poétiques* (1820) was an immediate success. Without discarding the Alexandrine line and Neo-Classical imagery still in vogue, he imparted to French poetry a musicality and lyricism it had lost for two centuries. The effect of Chateaubriand on the new poet was obvious. Many felt modern Christian poetry had come into its own.

III *Marriage and Promising Career*

Definitely on the road to a successful career, Lamartine acquired a great deal of stability in his personal life by marrying an accomplished English lady, Marianne Birch, in 1823. In the 1820's he produced further works, the *Chant du sacre, Mort de Socrate, Nouvelles Méditations,* and the *Dernier Chant du pèlerinage d'Harold.* At the same time, he entered the diplomatic service as secretary to the French embassy in Naples and Florence. At the end of the decade the *Harmonies poétiques et religieuses* (1830) appeared.

Lamartine now had his mind set on a political career. A period in the diplomatic service qualified him for public office, but Lamartine wisely chose to acquire further background. Since Chateaubriand profited by visiting the Near East and writing an account of his travels, Lamartine planned a similar trip. He set out for Palestine in 1832. At Beirut his only child, Julia, died. (Previously the Lamartines had lost an infant son.) Grief-stricken the poet returned to France to fill the post created for him in his absence when the department of the Nord elected him to the Chamber of Deputies.

Although by 1839 he had published the *Voyage en orient, Jocelyn, La Chute d'un ange,* and *Recueillements poétiques,* politics absorbed much of his time. He entered the Chamber not long after the establishment of the July Monarchy. Louis-Philippe had the support of big business, and "Get rich!" became the slogan of his government. Unrest characterized much of Louis-Philippe's reign with attempted assassinations and leftist agitation. Law and order were an issue, and repressive legislation gave France the appearance of a police state. Popular approval mattered little since the king had only to please the *pays légal*, the minority that had the right to vote. The ministry alternated between Adolphe Thiers and François Guizot. Louis-Philippe established a majority in the Chamber with ease. Deputies received no pay, so the membership came from the wealthy usually favorable to the king.

IV   *Career in Politics*

Many problems plagued the July Monarchy—war and peace, labor unrest, Church-state relations, and free trade. There was a bold search for new values resulting from the restless spirit of Romanticism. George Sand depicted the plight of the unliberated female. Songs popular among the workers echoed the utopian ideas of reformers. The working class was to provide much of the impetus for the Revolution of 1848.[2]

Such was the political situation facing Lamartine in the Chamber. With his poetic gifts, he could compose lofty speeches on the spur of the moment. Ladies attended sessions to catch a glimpse of the poet and lover of Julie and Graziella. Lamartine in his own accounts gives the impression his eloquence often moved implacable foes to kiss his hand following a stirring address. Opponents had the opposite impression. When Lamartine rose to speak it was the signal to read newspapers and to suppress yawns. Many accused him of an overbearing egotism and of a gross oversimplification of complex issues.

Like any political novice Lamartine made mistakes, but he soon realized the strengths and weaknesses of his position. He already enjoyed the confidence of monarchists and Catholics owing to his family background. Gradually he adopted a liberal attitude toward social problems. In general he opposed a foreign policy that would lead to war. A friend of religious values, he favored freeing the Church from any ties to the state. Lamartine's speeches were sufficiently ambiguous and varied to please most of the different political groups, each one interpreting his statements in light of its own persuasion.

Aware of this broad appeal, Lamartine played his part carefully. After 1843 he absented himself frequently from the Chamber and delivered few speeches. Already in 1840 he hinted that he was biding his time. Five years before the revolution he predicted almost to the day the moment when both the Right and Left would proclaim him their leader. His isolation from the main political parties fascinated the public. With the publication of the *Histoire des Girondins,* he became one of the leading political figures in France.

V *Brief Period of Glory*

No severe outbreak was anticipated in February, 1848. There had been a series of political banquets in protest against Louis-Philippe's government and an economic slump whose outcome was not foreseen. The king had aged and was less astute in judgment. Few, except Lamartine and the leftists, realized the growing discontent of Parisian workers. When Lamartine openly attacked the regime of Louis-Philippe in the Chamber, the end was near. Public demonstrations obliged the king to form a new ministry. This failed, and on February 24, 1848, Louis-Philippe abdicated. Lamartine, as minister of foreign affairs, headed the new government. France was once again a democratic state. Now at the height of his popularity, Lamartine appeared seven times on the balcony of the Hôtel de Ville to assure the populace there was a republic. The word "republic" became a handy shibboleth to Lamartine by enabling him to placate Socialists without any explicit commitment to radicalism. Conservatives accepted, for the moment, a republic as a preferable alternative to a proletarian regime. All groups were represented on the executive committee of the provisional government, and for a time Lamartine's ambivalent pronouncements stood him in good stead. His oratory and success in calming mobs made him seem the hero of a Romantic drama. He had wide support in rejecting an Orleanist regency. Refusal to accept the red flag of socialism and retention of the republican tricolor allayed the fears of moderates and conservatives. Reckless in exposing himself to possible assassination, he gave proof of personal courage. France witnessed a rare spectacle—a liberal poet swept into power by a revolution. It was a historical event unknown in European history.

All Europe was viewing France with alarm. Monarchs feared

another aggressive revolutionary government in Paris and talked
seriously of armed intervention. Revolts broke out in Poland and
Italy, where supporters of the revolts looked to France for aid.
Lamartine's most significant act was to ensure the peace by not
sending French troops to support rebellion elsewhere. Polish
and Italian nationals in Paris furiously demanded that France
fight Russia and Austria.

Minor protests, at first, did little to undermine Lamartine.
Colleagues on the executive committee, though not always in
agreement, accepted his leadership. On April 26, 1848, he mobilized the National Guard to thwart an uprising with no loss of
support. Shortly afterward on April 27 he received an over-
whelming vote of confidence and was in a position to assume
a virtual dictatorship. Instead Lamartine chose the opposite
course by deliberately backing policies counter to the wishes
of the country at large. France was still basically conservative,
and three quarters of the nation consisted of peasants opposed
to sweeping changes. With complete disregard of the political
realities, Lamartine advocated a continuance of public work
projects subsidized by the government and other forms of social
welfare. His refusal to dismiss Ledru-Rollin, too liberal in the
conservatives' estimation, cost him some votes in the election
of a commission to replace the provisional government.

With the signs of hostile reaction to socialism setting in, the
workers, already armed, collected weapons and erected barri-
cades. Previously Lamartine had called up the National Guard
halfheartedly but was finally obliged to speak firmly of the use
of force. General Louis Cavaignac took command of the army in
Paris. Some accused Cavaignac of deliberately delaying any
move against the rebels in order to topple the executive commission. Cavaignac denied these charges on military grounds;
there were not, he maintained, enough troops to storm the bar-
ricades that lined Paris streets. Frustrated by a debate over the
proper use of force, the commission resigned on June 24, 1848,
in favor of a temporary dictatorship under Cavaignac. With the
harsh suppression of the workers' uprising, Lamartine faded in
importance. Louis-Napoleon became the symbol of law and order,
and in December, 1848, decisively defeated Lamartine and other
opponents in the presidential election. The poet's fall from

power was as dramatic as his rise to prominence. His home district of Mâcon did not return him to the Chamber in 1849. He required another district to send him back for a brief period as a deputy.

VI *Defeat and Oblivion*

Various theories exist concerning Lamartine's role in 1848. To some he was merely a bungler who failed when his luck ran out. Karl Marx accused him of being an undercover agent for the capitalists in a plot to exploit the proletariat. Admirers considered him nothing less than a tragic hero who fought against insuperable odds. The truth, perhaps, would substantiate neither extreme praise nor censure. He was not the tool of big business and lacked the heroic proportions of a figure in classical tragedy. Still he was in all probability sincere in his efforts to effect an easy transition from the July Monarchy to the Second Republic. At the risk of his political future, he sought to improve the lot of the average worker. Peace was preserved in Europe through his refusal to intervene in revolutions outside France. To the best of his ability he tried to avert a bloody clash between the army and rebellious laborers.

Creditors besieged Lamartine following his downfall. He had kept an expensive apartment in Paris to entertain leading figures of the day. He was now obliged to live more modestly. His wife remained by his side in the gloomy period when he was reduced to hack writing to pay off debts. Lamartine wrote a series of histories on France, Turkey, and Russia. In 1856 he commenced the *Cours familier de littérature,* a miscellany of twenty-eight volumes on a variety of topics.

The daily routine of the poet changed drastically. Crowds occasionally would cheer him when he was seen in public, but by and large he was ignored except by critics who jeered at his misfortune. Close friends did not abandon him; they enjoyed talking to Lamartine. His conversations were ironic or sentimental as the mood struck him. Much of his time was spent in writing. For years he had been accustomed to rising at four in the morning to work on a manuscript. Owing to financial pressures, this effort had to be increased. He alternated his residence

between the family estate at Saint-Point and a chalet near the
Bois de Boulogne in Paris provided for him by Napoleon III.
When the sultan of Turkey offered him some land, he made
another trip to the East to inspect it.

At Saint-Point he had occasion to forget literary and political
concerns in hunting and caring for his dogs of which he was
very fond. Lamartine prided himself on his ability to judge
horses, a claim belied by the sorry-looking nags in his stable.
His financial insights were little better, and money problems
beset him to the end. At first he refused any help from Napoleon
III but at last accepted a pension. A niece, Valentine de Cessiat,
took charge of the poet's household after the death of Madame
Lamartine in 1863. He suffered in his final months from a crip-
pling rheumatism and died in 1869 in the Church, a fact still the
subject of speculation. Only a few persons attended his funeral.
Many in their twenties would have sneered at Lamartine even
at his grave. Only some time after his demise was it once more
fashionable to read the *Méditations*.

VII   *Lamartine's Outlook on Religion and Philosophy*

During the early 1800's at Belley, Lamartine was exposed to
several religious and philosophical points of view. Voltaire
still had his admirers, and Rousseau even to practicing Catholics
seemed a defender of religion. His mother was as much a disciple
of the Vicaire Savoyard as a follower of Rome. The validity of
Catholic claims to divine origins appeared substantiated by
Chateaubriand's stress on the beauty of Church liturgy and
customs. Owing to Cousin's revival of interest in the Greek
philosopher, Platonism in the 1820's was in the air. Hinduism
was also a topic of conversation, and Friedrich Creuzer's work on
India was widely read.[3] An especially intriguing ideological
undercurrent was the persistence of theosophy, which emphasized man's ability to obtain through natural means a form of
direct revelation from the deity. Louis-Claude de Saint-Martin
was particularly attractive to writers seeking a form of mysticism
free of the formalism of organized religion.[4] In touch with these
currents, Lamartine was to attempt to fuse them all into a system
of his own. Such was the spirit of the times when Victor Cousin

through his school of Eclecticism sought truth in all beliefs no matter how divergent. Affected by this very spirit, the poet expressed in his lyrics a viewpoint compounded of Catholicism, Platonism, rationalism, Martinism, and Hinduism.[5]

LAMARTINE

CHAPTER 2

From the Méditations to the Harmonies

I Early Attempts at the Theater

SAÜL was composed in 1817 but was not published in complete form until 1861 by Didot.

Lamartine intended to have François Joseph Talma play the title role in the drama. Talma, leading tragedian of the time and innovator in costuming and scenery, politely declined the offer without specifying his reasons, although they would seem obvious enough upon reading the play.

The story briefly is as follows. David, previously banished by Saul, returns and is welcomed by Micole, his wife and daughter of Saul, and her brother Jonathan. When Saul learns from Achimdech that David will succeed him, he orders the high priest's execution. The Philistines attack, and Jonathan, mortally wounded, meets his father on the battlefield. Jonathan expires after asking pardon for David and Saul, grief-stricken, stabs himself. As the king lies dying, David returns from a victory over the Philistines.

The play represents a feeble attempt to imitate Racine and Corneille. There are Shakespearean elements—the appearance of Samuel's ghost and the setting in the Jewish camp before the battle with the Philistines. Parts of Saül parallel the Méditations written concurrently. The Bible becomes a source of inspiration for the poet. God is the vindictive deity of Le Désespoir, and many of the lines, like those of the Méditations, represent an attempt to recapture the tone and rhythm of the Psalms. Saül also serves to emphasize the young Lamartine's classical leanings. The long dull tirades, however, display little of the musicality that was to delight a new generation of readers.

Both plays Médée and Zoraïde were published in 1873 in the Poésies inédites. They were written in 1813, but the original

manuscripts were lost. With *Saül* they provide evidence of
Lamartine's early ambition to be a playwright.

   Médée follows the main outlines of the legend except that
Jason's rejected wife does not kill Creon, the king of Athens.
Lamartine's Medea does slay her two sons by Jason when she
learns of her husband's plans to marry the princess of Athens.
   In *Zoraïde* the central problem is not revenge but religious
intolerance. Lamartine finished only the first two acts, but they
suffice to give some idea of the lines along which the play might
have been developed. Zoraide finds Antioch besieged by Con-
rad, her Christian lover. He sneaks into the city in disguise to see
her. Apprehended by her father, the Moslem ruler Osmin, Con-
rad is thrown into a dungeon.
   A reading of *Médée* and *Zoraïde* is sufficient to prove the wis-
dom of Lamartine's decision to abandon the theater. The boring
and lengthy discourses in *Médée* have none of Racine's brilliant
diction. An attempt to imitate Shakespeare, when Medea bran-
dishes her bloody dagger, borders on the ludicrous.
   Zoraïde brings to mind Voltaire's *Alzire* with its theme of
tolerance amidst Christian and Moslem antagonism. It serves
perhaps as early evidence that Lamartine's Catholicism was not
narrowly dogmatic. More important are the indications in both
plays of Lamartine's fondness for the theater and taste for the
melodramatic, a phase passed through by Stendhal, Mérimée,
and other Romantics in their early years.

II   Méditations poétiques

   The *Méditations poétiques* was published in March, 1820,
by Didot. Twenty-four poems made up the collection whose
contents justified the title. From the first poem, "L'Isolement" to
the last, "La Poésie sacrée," a general plan was discernible.
Starting on a reflective tone, the work depicted various stages of
religious feelings and attitudes and ended in a hymn of praise.
Lamartine preached to the skeptical Byron, underwent momentary doubts followed by a rebirth of faith, presented his own
version of mystical experience, and pondered on various aspects
of nature, humanity, and the universe.[1]
   Throughout the *Méditations* Lamartine assumed a personalized

tone. Yet structurally his work represented no sharp break with Classicism. The Alexandrine or twelve-syllable line divided into hemistichs, or divisions of six lines with a caesura, was preserved in the main. Nor was the imagery calculated to startle contemporary readers used to the poetry of Jacques Delille and Charles Chênedollé. Much of the *Méditations* smacked of the Neo-Classical vogue of the Empire with a fresh element injected. The *Génie du Christianisme* had unmistakably left its mark on Lamartine, and many lines recalled the cadenced prose of Chateaubriand. Fondness for the natural world, its trees, hills, lakes, and forests, represented nothing surprisingly new. Lamartine, however, made use of this background to insert an intensely personal note into his lyrics in which nature literally seemed to vibrate in sympathy with the poet. The *Méditations* was especially relevant to the younger generation of the 1820's, reared in the tradition of Rousseau's sentimentalism and the religious emotionalism of Chateaubriand. Lamartine's brand of poetry and mysticism blended admirably with the scheme of things. Little wonder then that his poems were read passionately to hushed audiences in the refined salons of the Romantic period.

Foreign sources were noticeably present in the *Méditations*. Brooding about man's existence, the origin of the soul, and other weighty questions brings to mind similar observations in Young's *Night Thoughts*, Gray's *Elegy*, and Pope's *Essay on Man*. Ossian and Petrarch also furnished themes employed by the poet, and there was a Byronic cast to many lines.

III   *Summary*

The opening poem, "L'Isolement," communicates to the reader the basic mood of the *Méditations*:

However, coming forth from the gothic spire, a religious sound is spread in the air; the wayfarer stops, and the rustic bell mingles holy music with the last sounds of the day.[2]

Lamartine subtly blends a natural setting with a religious motif in the manner of Chateaubriand without accumulating a series of concrete terms the Classicist would judge in bad taste.

The soft, flowing quality of Lamartine's verse marked its freshness despite its Neo-Classical form.

In "L'Homme" Lamartine took on the task of reminding his cynical colleague, Byron, of man's sublime destiny: "Limited in his nature, infinite in his aspirations, man is a fallen god who recalls the heavens."[3]

The Platonic commonplace of the soul's preexistence supplies a transcendental concept of man's immortality based on a spiritual destination beyond this earth where after death the soul will be reunited with the perfection that is God. Christianizing a Platonic notion dates back to Augustine, but Lamartine reintroduces it here in the context of Romantic individualism and the quest of an ideal order. Lecturing to Byron on the necessity of leading a Christian life impressed Catholic readers, but the English poet cursed the French writer's presumptuousness.

With the remonstrance to Byron out of the way, he again invokes a reflective mood in "Le Soir": "The evening brings back silence. Seated upon these forsaken rocks, I follow in the open sky the nocturnal chariot that is approaching."[4]

The octosyllabic quatrain, a standard form in the eighteenth century, denotes the extent of Lamartine's Classical roots. In this type of stanza there was greater freedom in placing the caesura. Ossianic themes, the starlight night and the invocation to the evening star, are present in "Le Soir." Lamartine belonged to a generation in which many still did not question the authenticity of Macpherson's translations of the Celtic bard.

"L'Immortalité" touches upon the subject of earthly love and asks whether two lovers separated in this life will be reunited in the next:

After a vain sigh, after the last farewell from all that [once] loved you, is there [now] no longer anything that does love you? Ah! only question yourself about this great secret! Behold the one who loves you dying, Elvire, and answer me![5]

Deprived of this theme, Romanticism would lack a vital element, one that permitted poets to unite the profane and the divine. Did not God, the exemplar of celestial love, smile upon its human manifestations? Lamartine asks this question of Elvire, a composite of Julie and Graziella who represented to Lamartine a latter-day version of Dante's Beatrice.

"Le Vallon," written in the same vein as "L'Isolement" and "Le Soir," affords a quiet broken by "Le Désespoir." Here Lamartine complains of a cruel and indifferent deity:

Heirs of sufferings, victims of life, no, don't expect His appeased rage to deaden [the pain of] Misfortune, until death, unfolding her enormous wing, swallows up forever eternal suffering in everlasting silence![6]

Seemingly Voltairean in tone, "Le Désespoir" has been a convenient point of departure for critics bent on making an agnostic out of Lamartine. Nothing could be further from the truth. The underlying motif, despite Voltairean rhetoric, is Jobean. Chateaubriand popularized the Bible, and the Book of Job with its strains of despair and melancholy was a favorite of the French Romantics. "Le Désespoir" is simply a literary convention and expresses the momentary doubts experienced by many believers. The next poem, "La Providence à l'homme," supplies a rebuttal by God Himself to the blasphemy of "Le Désespoir":

What! the son of the void has cursed existence! What! You can accuse me of my own good deeds. You can close your eyes to the magnificence of the gifts I have bestowed on you![7]

From this point on in the *Méditations* Lamartine no longer questions God's will and returns to more tranquil themes. "Souvenir" is another graceful poem striking a meditative mood in which the poet muses on the passage of time. The calmness of "Souvenir" yields to a more vigorous tempo in "L'Enthousiasme" and the expressed desire to love in the present rather than indulge in a fruitless quest for fame:

Glory is the dream of a shadow. It has reduced too much the number of days on which it should cast its spell. You want me to sacrifice to it this last breath of my life! I wish to keep it in order to love.[8]

The motif of the preceding lines supplies a fitting introduction to "Le Lac," the most popular and best-known poem of the

Méditations. Scenes from *Atala* and the *Nouvelle Héloïse* are recalled more than once in the description of two lovers enthralled by the beauty of the lake and the forest. The passage of time is a phenomenon that perplexes Lamartine and Elvire:

Eternity, nothingness, past, sombre abysses, what do you do with the days you engulf? Speak, will you give back to us these sublime ecstasies that you snatch from us?[9]

There is little question that "Le Lac" records the poet's vivid recollections of moments spent with Julie Charles in a similar setting. Rousseau had already popularized the theme of "Le Lac," namely, the return to a spot that recalls passionate and tender memories of bygone days. Sénancour in *Obermann* and Byron in *Childe Harold* employed a similar technique. Lamartine was acquainted with these sources as well as with Rousseau. In fact, this particular theme can be traced back to the pastoral novel of the seventeenth century.

Joined to the motif of a return to a place where love knew brighter moments is the concept of the impermanence of time, its fleeting character and instability. Besides Rousseau, Mme de Staël also favored this notion of the passage of time as a poetic theme which was counterbalanced by the knowledge that eternity would provide the repose incapable of realization in this life. Ossian, as interpreted by Macpherson, would have furnished Lamartine the idea of the appeal to nature to perpetuate the memory of his love for Julie.

At the time "Le Lac" was composed Julie was still alive. Her subsequent death gave an entirely different meaning to the original lines, which understandably became more touching and tragic. Even in reading the poem with the knowledge it was written before Julie had died many still receive the impression that Lamartine somehow had a premonition of impending tragedy.

In the ephemeral aspect of time the poet also touches upon a theme familiar to the great writers of French Classicism. Certainly Pascal dwelt upon the transitory character of earthly existence in stressing the need for man to focus his thoughts on eternity. Bossuet, for that matter, frequently referred to the

same theme in his sermons. An admirer of the Classicists, Lamartine learned many a valuable lesson from them. By that token
"Le Lac," then, embraces themes common to several literary
schools. It is consequently all the more remarkable that Lamartine gave fresh life to what was by 1820 a literary convention.

With an abrupt switch in tempo and subject Lamartine dedi-
cates the eleventh meditation, "La Gloire," to a Portuguese writer,
Manuel do Nascimento. It is a sober piece written with a Neo-
Classical flourish possibly intended to please conservative read-
ers who would not quite condone the passionate emotions in
"Le Lac."

The twelfth meditation, "La Prière," has not always received
the attention it deserves. Lamartine prized it highly as an expression of poetry in the highest sense of the term. All nature joins
the poet in adoration of God:

Behold the immense, universal sacrifice! The universe is the temple
and the earth is the altar. The heavens are the dome, and these
stars without number, pale ornament of the shadow, sown with
order in the azure archway, are the sacred candles lit for this
temple. . . .[10]

This passage has Martinist overtones with its comparison of a
natural setting to a cathedral. As in the Catholic mass the candles
are lit and the altar ready. The poet himself acts as priest, thus
completing Louis-Claude de Saint-Martin's prescription for
worship of God in nature. According to Martinist teaching a
select group, the *hommes de désir* (men of desire), possessed
extraordinary insights into the divine will and plan. Their duty
was to make this revelation known to other men. Lamartine
adapted this concept to the Romantic notion of the poet's lofty
mission. The *homme de désir* of Saint-Martin becomes the poet
in his exercise of a sacerdotal function. As the poet-priest Lamartine communicates with a deity who transcends sectarian
bounds: "Soul of the universe, God, Father, Creator. Under these
divine names, I believe in you, Lord. . . ."[11]

In the performance of his priestly office, Lamartine composes
a prayer embracing some of the major religious beliefs held by
mankind—deistic, pantheistic, and Christian. With his easygoing
approach to theology, the poet probably felt the prayer was

sufficiently Christianized by using *Seigneur* (Lord) as a common denominator. It is also a reflection of Eclecticism, the school established by Victor Cousin, and a trend that affected Lamartine's thinking.

"La Prière" was for the author the high point of the *Méditations* although readers undoubtedly enjoyed shorter selections like "Invocation" where the poet dreamed of a Platonic reunion in the next world with Elvire.

"La Foi" rejects all obstacles to belief and, putting aside rationalistic arguments on God's existence, relies on intuition to attain knowledge of the deity much in the manner of the Vicaire Savoyard: "This proud reason, an insufficient light, is extinguished, as life is, at the doors of the tomb. . . ."[12]

The "Golfe de Baïa" relieves the reader temporarily of theological concerns as Lamartine gives vent to his antiquarian interests by singing the praises of ancient Rome's architectural achievements. Then "Le Temple" marks a return to Catholic motifs, the Church and its spiritual consolation being detailed in the best Chateaubriandesque fashion.

The "Chants lyriques de Saül" represents Lamartine's effort to capture some of the solemnity of the Psalms. At times he has fair success in simulating the psalmist's loftiness of tone: "God! How sweet the air is! How pure the light! You reign as victor over all nature."[13]

The "Hymne au soleil" and "Adieu" recapitulate, respectively, the reunion of lovers in a Platonic paradise and the poet's farewell to the world. Lamartine handles such themes well but is more at home in "La Semaine sainte" recording his impressions of worshipers during the final week of Lent:

All these bowed foreheads, this fire which sets them aglow, these perfumes, these sighs being exhaled from the holy place, this passionate enthusiasm, these tears of ecstasy, all reply to me that there is a God.[14]

Quite fittingly the "Chrétien mourant" enlarges on the message of "La Semaine sainte" since the devout Christian must eventually resign himself to death. Much of the poem has a ring of sincerity because Lamartine wrote it when he was very ill. The same quality is discernible in "Dieu" as the poet makes another Platonic analysis of the soul's origin and destiny. For an indication of Lamartine's attitude toward nature, "L'Automne" furnishes a handy example. Under his pen the scene acquires some of the light and color imparted by eighteenth-century landscapists to their paintings:

Earth, sun, valleys, beautiful and sweet nature, I owe you a tear at the edge of my grave. The air is so fragrant, the light is so pure! The sun is so beautiful to the eyes of a dying man.[15]

From the serenity of "L'Automne" Lamartine moves on to the final poem, "La Poesie sacrée." Having sung the divine praises, the poet bids his muse be still as he awaits the coming of the Lord:

Silence, o lyre, [be] you silent, prophets, voices of the future! All the universe in advance grows still before the one who is to come![16]

IV *Evaluation*

Thus the *Méditations* opens and closes with a note of prayer and contemplation which outwardly at least justified the title of a work that created a sensation on the Paris bookmarket. Lamartine managed to combine various elements that would guarantee a wide readership during the Restoration. Devotees of Chateaubriand and Rousseau could not fail to be moved by the sentimental mixture of profane and divine love set against a backdrop of beautiful, placid lakes and majestic forests. The Christian cast of many of the poems convinced all but the most scrupulous theologians that the *Méditations* was the poetic counterpart of the prose masterpiece, the *Génie du Christianisme*. Without offending Neo-Classical sensibilities, Lamartine brought a new spirit to the French lyric. No radical departure from standard versification, subject matter, and vocabulary was necessary to allow a poet with a fresh view of God and nature to instill new life into French poetry. The *Méditations* remains today—despite changing literary fads—one of the landmarks in French literature. Unquestionably, modern poetry owes much to Lamartine, the first widely read poet since the Pléiade to restore personalism as a necessary component of the lyric. Debates may continue on the significance and merits of that contribution, but the issue seems to narrow down to whether Lamartine was a great poet or just a good one. In view of his mastery of the idyllic setting and the sheer musicality of poems like *Le Lac*, he does not deserve neglect.

V   Nouvelles Méditations

The *Nouvelles Méditations* was published in 1823 by Canel. Many of the poems repeated themes of the *Premières Méditations*. "L'Esprit de Dieu" resembled "La Foi." "Sapho" bore a Classical stamp, and "La Solitude" was reminiscent of "L'Isolement."

One of the most widely read poems, not only in France but in England and America, was "Bonaparte." In reviewing Napoleon's career the poet in spite of Bourbonist leanings left final judgment of the erstwhile usurper to God:

His coffin is closed. God judged him. Silence! His crime and his exploits weigh in the balance. Let the hand of weak mortals touch it no more! Who can fathom, Lord, your infinite clemency? And you, scourges of God, who knows whether genius is not one of your virtues?[17]

For the first time in his writing Lamartine openly touched upon political and social issues. The Bonapartist cause was not dead, and Lamartine might well be addressing Napoleon's sympathizers when he describes how peaceful France would have been if their hero had restored the Bourbons to power. Tyrants, however, forget how they will ultimately appear in God's eyes.

Similarly in "La Liberté" when he considers Rome's past he reflects on the dangers of anarchy: "When the people are the tyrant, they insult kings!"[18] Without doubt, the poet was thinking of the violence of the French Revolution and may have sensed he would one day be in a similar position.

One short poem, "Le Papillon," provided a pleasant contrast to Lamartine's customary lyrics. The butterfly flitting about becomes a symbol of the poet seeking eternal truth:

To be intoxicated with fragrance, light and the azure sky shaking, still young, the powder from its wings. To take flight like a breath of air towards the eternal heavens. Behold the enchanted destiny of the butterfly.[19]

Lamartine's occasional use of one symbol as the central motif of a poem suggests that in some way he foreshadowed the more sophisticated techniques of the Symbolists. "La Branche d'amandier," for example, centers the reader's attention on a flower signifying the fleeting delights of life here on earth:

Blossoming trunk of the almond-tree, symbol, alas, of beauty. Like you the flower of life blossoms and falls before summer.[20]

The writer compares himself in "Le Poète mourant" to migratory birds who never linger long enough in one spot to make a lasting impression on those who have heard their song:

The poet is like the migratory birds, who do not build their nests on the shore, who do not place themselves on the branches of the trees. Nonchalantly cradled on the current of the wave, they pass singing far from the shores and the world knows nothing about them except their voice.[21]

If Lamartine dealt on occasion with art and life in simple direct symbols unobscured by literary artifices, he was equally forthright in acknowledging, as he does in "Les Préludes," his basically rural orientation:

Yes, I return to you, cradle of my childhood, to embrace forever your protecting hearths. [Keep] far from me cities and their vain opulence. I was born among the shepherds.[22]

The Lamartine who wrote these lines was a lover of the outdoors and numbered many dogs and horses among his pets. He was a man of action still capable of reflections almost feminine in their sensitivity in "Le Crucifix" such as the scene where the priest administers the Last Sacrament to Julie Charles:

The holy candles cast a final glow. The priest murmured these soft chants of the dead similar to the plaintive songs which a woman whispers to the child who is falling asleep.[23]

All the familiar ingredients used so well by Lamartine are here, the moving ceremonial of the Church, the paternal figure of the priest, and the prayers for the dying. He combines them effectively in commemorating the death of Julie Charles. Although the poet exalts an adulterous love, readers at the time applauded this deft mixture of the profane and divine. In heaven lovers, married or not, would be reunited. Many concurred with Lamartine in this belief that love would be thus raised to a higher level. In no other poem did he blend so successfully current secular and religious tastes. Sentimental Christianity was present, and the poet like Chactas mourned the death of his sweetheart. For popular consumption it was a most workable formula. Lamartine enjoyed a reputation with the public as a Christian poet. The opinion of theologians in the seminaries, therefore, mattered little.

Besides the continued use of devices that assured the initial success of the *Méditations,* the *Nouvelles Méditations* introduces new features in Lamartine's writing. Political and social issues begin to form part of his perspective and he utilizes on occasion a central image in a poem. His verse was still basically Neo-Classical in structure, and he desired no rupture with standard verse form. Equally concerned about traditional religious ties, he had no quarrel with the Church although he was by no means a dogmatist as is borne out by the profane spirit of "Le Crucifix." Even here he was not an intractable rebel. Catholic poets before him had freely intermingled the theme of love of God and that of comely lasses without being excommunicated.

VI La Mort de Socrate

La Mort de Socrate was published in 1823 by Hatier. The subject, a popular one in the eighteenth century, attracted Rousseau who compared Socrates' death to the crucifixion of Christ. Lamartine also likens the demise of Socrates to Jesus' sacrifice and in so doing has him foretell to his pagan brethren the advent of the one true God:

Just a little while longer, and your great crowd receding with the error of your crumbling olympus will give way to the one, holy, universal God, the only God I adore and who has no altar.[24]

The last line has been interpreted by some as a rationalistic remark, although, since Lamartine sees Socrates here as an ally of Christ, emphasis is probably being placed on the nonpagan manner in which the new, unknown god is to be worshiped. The poet was more concerned with finding a common ground for Platonism and Christianity. Accordingly, he pictures the soul of Socrates in a place where the Platonic World of Ideas and the Christian heaven are one and the same:

Seeking these great spirits it had formerly loved, from sun to sun, from system to system it flies and loses itself with the soul that it loves, follows the vast detours of infinite space, and in the bosom of God always finds itself again![25]

Lamartine's Socrates is also a true Romantic in the nineteenth-century sense. Life to him seems at best a melancholy affair on this earth and serves largely as a form of expiation: "Life is the struggle, death is the victory and earth is for us the expiatory altar...."[26]

La Mort de Socrate, in a period when Platonism and Eclecticism were in vogue, catered to contemporary tastes and enhanced Lamartine's status as poet-philosopher. Academicians would dispute this claim, but their opinion had little effect on the sale of Lamartine's works. Not read much today, *La Mort de Socrate* is merely a mediocre piece of poetry of interest only as an indication of the range of the poet's subject matter.

VII   Le Chant du sacre

Le Chant du sacre, published in 1825 by Baudouin, gave Lamartine an opportunity to air his Bourbonist views. Written on the occasion of Charles X's coronation, it depicted the new king as a successor to the ancient paladins of France. In the poem Charles X keeps vigil through the night awaiting the solemn moment of coronation. After placing the crown upon Charles' head the archbishop tells him that, unlike people in medieval times, no one expected supernatural manifestations to accompany great events. Instead the modern era looks upon great men as a sign from heaven:

But the times are no more! The past removes them. Heaven speaks
to the earth a stronger language. It is reason alone which explains it
to faith. Great events, there are the great wonders![27]

More than likely Lamartine was merely toadying to the newly
crowned king and not making a disparaging remark about
Church teaching on miracles. Catholicism still satisfied his
emotional needs; moreover, he had other preoccupations,
chief of which was a contemplated career as diplomat and states-
man. A role as singer of royal praises would not diminish his
chances. Certainly *Le Chant du sacre* had to serve some purpose.
It did nothing for his literary reputation.

VIII   Le Dernier Chant du pèlerinage d'Harold

Le Dernier Chant was published in 1825 by Dondey-Dupré.
Byron had died in Greece the previous year, and Lamartine felt
impelled to write another poem like "L'Immortalité" dedicated
to the English poet and which would narrate the final events
in Byron's life. Harold's skepticism is in reality Byron's own
cynicism about religion in general: "Jupiter, Mohammed, heroes,
great men, gods, O Christ, pardon him, are nothing in his
eyes. . . ."[28]
Always fond of listing the major world religions, Lamartine
has a field day in treating Harold's peculiar system of meta-
physics, which takes a rather cold view of the world and its
Creator:

The God that Harold adores is this supreme agent, this mysterious
Pan, an insoluble problem, great, limited, good, bad, which this vast
universe reveals to his eyes under a thousand different aspects. A
being without attributes, a force without providence, exercising by
chance a blind power. . . .[29]

A penchant for involvement with philosophical concepts when
writing poetry makes Lamartine subject to various interpretations at times. Harold's lack of a firm belief in a divinity as
described here by Lamartine does not signify a continuation of
the skepticism of "Le Désespoir." The poet simply sets the mood
for the final phase of the poem where Harold, after wandering

through the world, dies, meets Christ face to face, and fails to
pass the test necessary to achieve salvation. Lamartine valued a
belief in a personal God and the hereafter. He somehow wished
Byron would share that belief. *Le Dernier Chant* was a vehicle
for Lamartine's religious notions as well as a means to take
advantage of the current Byronic craze in France. Having
achieved fame with the *Méditations poétiques* and the *Nouvelles
Méditations*, Lamartine temporarily lapsed into mediocrity. *Le
Chant du sacre, Le Mort de Socrate* and *Le Dernier Chant* attest
to that.

IX   Harmonies poétiques et religieuses

The *Harmonies poétiques et religieuses* was published in 1830
in Brussels by Michel. Since then there have been several
editions. Observing in the preface that some people by temperament were better suited to contemplation. Lamartine hinted
strongly he was one of the favored few and promised to depict
in the *Harmonies* the various mental and emotional states experienced in meditating on God and the wonders of the universe.

One of the first selections, "Invocation," a description of the
poet's role in offering to God his own homage and that of
nature, tells how his whole being trembles in the realization the
poetic gift is of divine origin:

But above all it is your name, O King of nature, which causes this
divine instrument to vibrate in me; when I invoke this name, my
heart filled with murmuring resounds like a temple where people
sing endlessly. ("Invocation")[30]

In fulfilling his function—the singing of the divine praises—
Lamartine contemplates the cosmos and is overwhelmed by the
evidence of God's omnipotence and omnipresence. He bids all
nature worship Him: "Carry back to the heavens the homage
of the dawn. Ascend, He is on high, descend, He is all!"[31]
("Hymne du Matin").

The poet's perspective is pantheistic in a general sense.
Everything is a reflection of God inasmuch as He exists everywhere. Lamartine does not speak of individual identity being
merged with a transcendent force in the world. Like most

Romantics, Lamartine is awed by the fact of divine ubiquity, and any expression of his wonderment is purely a literary tour de force; no metaphysical probing into God's nature is intended.

It was a different matter when a question of the believer's personal relationship with God. Every seeker after truth obtained a hearing from God whether Christian or Moslem:

In the absence of enlightenment, He credits us with a wish. The voice that cries "Allah!" the voice that says "My father!" bring to Him pure incense and false incense. [It is] for Him alone to choose. ("Aux Chrétiens")[32]

Basically nonsectarian in outlook, Lamartine went beyond doctrinal differences to embrace all believers in his world view. The preceding lines, often misread, do not reveal at an early date Lamartine's preference for Islamism, as some critics feel. They merely represent the poet's plea for tolerance on the part of fellow Christians.

If open-mindedness is necessary in assessing the sincerity of contemporary world religions, then it is even more so in any judgment of past theologies. The remains of great faiths of antiquity bear witness to man's endless desire to honor the deity:

Uncertain relics of an unremembered past. Mysteries of an old world written in mysteries. And you temples [still] standing, superb basilicas whose squares are animated by a divine breath! ("Jéhova")[33]

Man's religious thinking is in a state of flux because truth by its very nature is constantly evolving:

Behold the truth! Each century in turn believes it lifts its veil and walks by its light, but the one that our ignorance worships today is tomorrow only a cloud; another is ready to shine forth! ("Novissima verba")[34]

Central to many poems of the *Harmonies* is the notion of a timeless religious drive in man. Lamartine repeatedly asserts various aspects of his relation to God. Creeds may be changed and modified, but one factor remains constant—an instinct in man that directs his thoughts and aspirations to the Creator:

"Everywhere I sought the God that I adore wherever the instinct led me . . ."[35] ("Pourquoi mon âme est-elle triste?")

Such searching may cause the soul to despair, but Lamartine finds solace in prayer, a logical solution for a poet to whom poetry and prayer are one. Toward the close of the *Hymne au Christ* and after reflections on Jesus' sublime message Lamartine reverts to childhood remembrances and longs for the consolations of the simple unquestioning faith he once knew: "For me, whether your name revives or succumbs, O God of my cradle be the God of my tomb! ("Hymne au Christ").[36]

Two characteristics of Lamartine are the cherished notion of a childhood faith and an impulse to return to an earlier pattern of feeling when life was less complex and he enjoyed the heartwarming experience of everyday life at Milly. Regression was typical of other French Romantics when recalling their youth and early loves. In Lamartine this inclination expresses itself in some of his finest and most moving verse.

A true picture of what Lamartine actually thought and felt about nature, the physical world around him, may be read in those lines when he recalls the scenes of boyhood and adolescence at Milly. There he spent his happiest years and there he wishes to be buried:

Dig for me in these fields the grave that I long for and this last furrow from which another life will spring. ("Milly, ou la Terre natale")[37]

There is nothing artificial in the poet's spontaneous reaction to a swallow gliding gracefully over the water, and he is capable of depicting such moments honestly and without affectation:

Behold the wandering swallow which skims with the end of its wing the sleeping waters of the marsh. Behold the child from the huts who gathers on the heath the fallen wood of the forests. ("Pensée des morts")[38]

The song of another bird, the nightingale, will unite, he hopes, with his own prayer in order that all God's creatures may join in praise of Him:

Oh! Combine your voice with mine! The same ear hears us, but your airborne prayer rises better to the heaven that awaits us. ("Au Rossignol")[39]

This closeness to nature makes the poet aware of its dynamism:

And I hear buzzing under the grass that I trample upon these waves of living beings that each furrow unfolds. Atoms animated by the divine breath! Each ray of daylight rises from it without end. ("L'infini dans les cieux")[40]

More expansive in conceiving nature than the *Méditations,* the *Harmonies* discloses Lamartine's response to the physical forces at work about him. Basically an unabashed lover of the outdoors, he has a fierce devotion to his native soil. He can capture the mood of a quiet moment in the wilderness or use a lone bird as the central image of a poem. Lamartine is attuned as well to the vitality he senses in the smallest blade of grass. Too often dismissed as an effeminate poet, he had a virile temperament beneath the deceptive softness of his style.

Vigor and virility characterize "Les Révolutions" as Lamartine, after reviewing outmoded religious and social institutions, proclaims the need for mankind to be constantly on the march to better the human condition:

March! Humanity does not live by one idea! It extinguishes each evening the one that has guided it, it lights another from the inextinguishable torch; like these dead dressed in their soiled attire, the [passing] generations take along from this world their clothing into the tomb! ("Les Révolutions")[41]

The eighteenth-century notion of indefinite progress is insufficient for man's needs without the moral strength of Christianity. It is for Christians to combine progress with their religious heritage in leading mankind forward under their banner: "Under yours, O Christians! Man in whom God works constantly changes in form and size" ("Les Révolutions").[42]

To readers of the *Harmonies,* Lamartine's increasing awareness of life about him is readily discernible. The poet has not only developed a greater appreciation of God and nature; he has also become more responsive to political and social issues.

"Les Révolutions" reveals the writer's outlook on the eve of his formal entry into politics. Up to this point he has only enunciated general principles. The time is not far off when he will have to furnish specific answers to some perplexing problems.

Just as every aspect of human endeavor corresponds to the universal search for religious truth, nature too discloses a unifying principle which Lamartine detects in the felicitous arrangement of the various levels of creation:

Holy and mysterious law! A melodious soul animates the whole universe; each being has its harmony, each star its spirit, each element its concerts. ("Désir")[43]

As a result of the infinite harmony perceived in the cosmos Lamartine feels the urge to proclaim the wonders of creation. A faculty within the poet directs him to laud the deity whose omnipotence is so apparent:

But the instinct that adores you has grown in my soul; henceforth it is the only one my life needs; it sees, it senses, it touches, it hears, it proclaims things from on high and its God from afar! ("Le Solitaire")[44]

A by-product of this perception of universal harmony is an arresting image emphasizing the essential unity of the world:

It was this great spirit, this universal soul which lived, which felt, which vegetated for it. A being almost divine for which it was the body, that activated all the springs of its inert mass. . . . ("Hymne de l'ange de la terre après la destruction du globe")[45]

The oneness of the world had long been a tenet of Indic philosophy, and Lamartine by his use of the preceding figure shows a probable borrowing from an early work on Hinduism, Friedrich Creuzer's *Symbolik* translated in French by Joseph Guigniaut as *Religions de l'Antiquité*. A colorful friend of Lamartine, the able Baron d'Eckstein, an associate of Creuzer and Guigniaut, might well have acquainted the poet with the French version of *Symbolik*. Creuzer was well known as an orientologist in Europe, and French intellectuals hailed Guigniaut's translation. It would have been difficult for Lamartine not to have heard of *Religions de l'Anitiquité.* His knowledge of Creuzer's work during the 1820's prior to the publication of the *Harmonies* would establish Lamartine's initial contact with Hinduism at a date thirty years earlier than the one generally accepted. Those favoring the later date base their judgment on the poet's discussion of India in the *Cours familier* and conclude that previous to the 1850's no substantial evidence exists of Lamartine's familiarity with Hinduism. The poet met Eckstein during the 1820's and must have read the latter's *Le Catholique*: in its pages there was frequent mention of Creuzer and Guigniaut and an open invitation to Lamartine to study the ancient literature of India. Associating the poet with Hinduism is not an idle assumption in view of the current European interest in the Vedas.[46]

Nor is there likewise any risk in presuming Lamartine's acquaintance with Louis-Claude de Saint-Martin, traces of whose theosophy already appear in the *Méditations.* Martinism and Hinduism would provide the poet with apt metaphors to describe a mystical encounter with divine secrets hidden from ordinary mortals:

If the letter of the great book of nature, imperceptible to your eyes, does not disclose it everywhere, ah! man is the supreme book. In the fibers of his very heart read mortals! there is a God! ("L'Humanité")[47]

In the theosophic jargon of Saint-Martin, the person initiated into celestial mysteries was the divine book revealing God's secrets to the rest of mankind. Such a person in contact with the deity could aspire to a fuller knowledge of the universe. Lamartine would naturally limit such a privilege to the poet already favored with this preternatural talent.

While Lamartine's preoccupations in the *Harmonies* were often religious and philosophical, he could also turn his attention to the dispassionate contemplation of beauty. Take, for example, a passage depicting the sculptural grace of a young maid, her body covered by long, flowing hair:

It is entwined like a necklace about the white neck it embraces. (It) comes down, winds, and proceeds to unfold upon a bosom where scarcely swell up two sources from which life is to flow in streams of love. ("L'Humanité")[48]

Through a concern with the plastic aspects of his word painting the poet anticipates the Parnassians. Usually not associated with that school, Lamartine was capable at times of achieving some of the same effects. The poet's scope was not necessarily limited to the poetry of ideas.

X *Conclusion*

To a greater extent than preceding works the *Harmonies* supplies readers with a well-rounded picture of Lamartine's versatility and the central religious and philosophical themes of Lamartine's poetry. Many elements represent a carryover from the *Méditations*, the emotional states characteristic of prayer, alternate moods of hope and despair, worship of God in the great outdoors, a nostalgic longing for the homestead, and an eclectic view of religion. Lamartine explores further the diversity of creation. Besides observing the flora and fauna around him, he focuses his attention on a historical perspective of man. Christianity is a sublime exemplar of truth but not its sole possessor. Involvement in the dynamic nature of religious truth leads directly into a consideration of man's social progress. Faced with complexity on all levels of creation, the poet finds a solution in the realization everything is animated by one principle. Without becoming openly pantheistic, Lamartine depicts the oneness of a multifaceted world in terms borrowed from Hinduism and Martinism. He thus persists in and enlarges upon his eclectic view of the world.

CHAPTER 3

Apex of Lamartine's Career

I Alleged Break with Catholicism

A YEAR after the first edition of the *Harmonies* in 1831,
Lamartine met an engaging rationalist, Jean-Marie Dargaud. Their meeting has often been considered a turning point
in the poet's attitude toward the Church on the basis of a chance
remark to Dargaud by Lamartine about giving little more than
lip-service to Catholicism. The poet, already planning a political
career, was rapidly acquiring a knack for double-talk, and at
bottom there was nothing really very new in what he told
Dargaud. In the *Harmonies* he espoused an undogmatic Christianity. It is too often forgotten that Lamartine was the celebrity
and Dargaud the nonentity, currying favor with the former.
On warm terms with the chatty freethinker, Lamartine never
fully divulged to him his private religious views, which were
not those of a cold and calculating rationalist.

The question is further complicated by a poem written in
1831 and which remained unpublished until 1942. "Rome" constituted a reply to Auguste Barthélemy, a satirist who attacked
Pius IX for reactionary policies. Lamartine countered with the
argument the papacy was a bastion of freedom in Italy:

Have you forgotten that if the hand of the brave still feels a heart
beating in enslaved Italy it is because the shadow of Rome is still
in its midst? ("Rome")[1]

An epilogue later appended to the original manuscript contains a rejection of Lamartine's initial statement. The papacy
now appears too burdened with temporal concerns to heed
the voice of the oppressed. Even then, "Rome" is far from
being a bitter anticlerical diatribe. Quite possibly there were

41

political reasons for writing the poem. Lamartine had much to gain by retaining his Catholic image without offending liberal supporters. Faced with this dilemma, he left "Rome" unpublished. The manuscript furnishes nonetheless evidence of the poet's view that Catholicism contributed to moral stability. No loquacious Dargaud could talk him out of this conviction.

II *Persistence of Martinism*

A poem published in 1832 in honor of Sir Walter Scott contained an unmistakably Martinist note when describing man's role in the revelation of divine secrets:

Behold man, behold the immortal pontiff! A pontiff that God made to render the altar fragrant, to snatch from the sphinx the word of nature, to cast His light into our obscure night, and to make us spell out, in these divine accents, this great book of destiny, whose meaning He alone has. ("Réponse aux adieux de Sir Walter Scott")[2]

The implications are obvious. The pontiff Lamartine refers to is the poet. Again he makes use of Saint-Martin's allusion to the theosophist's priestly functions to depict the sublimity of the poetic calling. Written about the time he was to enter the Chamber of Deputies it reveals the mystical significance Lamartine probably attributed to his role in literature and politics, a role that in his own mind set him apart from ordinary men.

III *"Sur la politique rationnelle"*

"Sur la politique rationnelle" was published in 1831 by Gosselin. The tract contains points subsequently developed in Lamartine's speeches and histories.

Society, the poet maintains, has passed through the stages of theocracy, tyranny, and monarchy, and is now in the evangelical era when the religious principle is dominant. Church and state must be separated without the weakening of the moral fiber of society. Everyone must enjoy equal rights. With the voice of conscience guiding men progress seemed assured, although there was always danger of another major war in Europe

or revolution in France. In the lofty tone so characteristic of
his poetry and orations, Lamartine concluded a society must be
built upon moral principles based on reason.

IV "*Des destinées de la poésie*"

The essay, "Des destinées de la poésie," was published in
Paris by Gosselin in 1834. It is of importance to those interested
in Lamartine's most explicit statement on the nature of poetry
and the poet's role.

Lamartine begins by declaring man the most baffling mystery
of the universe. All of man's attempts to control his own destiny
have been in vain. After a consideration of man's need to rely
on God, the poet recalls the efforts in the eighteenth century
to discredit religion and the subsequent reaction against extreme rationalism led by Madame de Staël and Chateaubriand.
De l'Allemagne taught the value of enthusiasm to art, and the
Génie du Christianisme stressed the role of Christianity in in-
spiring artistic creativity. These two precursors initiated Lamartine into the secrets of poetic inspiration.

On the question of defining poetry, Lamartine hesitates to
give a definition of what is the most intimate and divine function of man's mind and heart. Poetry embodies at once both
idea and feeling and when properly expressed overwhelms the
poet with its sudden and immediate revelation. So staggering
is the moment of inspiration that even the greatest poet could
not compose indefinitely at one time. The reason for this awesome power lies in the source—God—and while the poet can
never rise to a level known only to the deity, he can catch a
glimpse of divine truth and transmit it to fellow men. Since
poetry comes from God, the voice of the poet will always be
heard and will reflect not only the poet's individual thoughts
but those of the society he represents.

In tracing the development of poetry, Lamartine refers to
his recent visit to the Near East. There he communed with
the past when gazing upon ancient monuments and imagining
the role of poets in antiquity. The Arabs especially impressed
Lamartine. A people dwelling in the wilderness where they
meditated on God, they exemplified the conditions under which

poetry first arose. With the modern era poetry had to meet a
new challenge. The traditional forms, epic, lyric, dramatic,
could no longer satisfy current and future demands of society.
Romantic theater was too vulgar to provide a worthy incentive.
What then did the future hold in store? Lamartine predicted:

Poetry will be reason voiced in song, behold its destiny for a long
time; it will be philosophical, religious, political, social, like the
periods mankind is going to pass through; it will be above all intimate,
personal, meditative, and solemn; no longer a witticism, a melodious
caprice of light and superficial thought, but the deep, real, sincere
echo of the loftiest conceptions of the mind, of the most mysterious
impressions of the soul. . . .[3]

Having rejected the witty but inconsequential verse often
associated with a decadent Classicism, Lamartine outlines a
concept of poetry of his own peculiar brand of Romanticism
wherein personalism and religious feeling are combined with a
growing social awareness. In the latter, Lamartine beholds the
future purpose of poetry as a mirror of the chief developments
in society. "Reason voiced in song" is the poetizing of the writer's
thoughts on the important issues of the day.

Lamartine refutes a major point of the "Préface de Cromwell"
by declaring Hugo's third stage in the development of poetry,
the drama, outmoded. The notion that poetry had a social
function was not unique, although Lamartine did give it fresh
emphasis. From "Des destinées de la poésie" there emerges a
fairly clear idea of Lamartine's concept of his own role. He
sincerely placed himself above ordinary mortals by reason of
the gift granted to him by God. The poetic process, he claimed,
could no more readily be defined than divine omnipotence. No
wonder Lamartine exasperated contemporaries with what they
deemed an overbearing egotism. Convinced he possessed a
preternatural talent, he assumed a lofty tone in his writings.
Martinism, with its emphasis on the extraordinary insights of
the theosophist, may well have strengthened this conviction.

Behind much of Lamartine's reasoning can be seen the effects
of a budding political career and a desire to enhance his public
image through an already established literary reputation. What

could be more logical for a poet, also a deputy in the Chamber, than to analyze his art in social and political terms?

V   Voyage en orient

On July 11, 1832, Lamartine left Marseilles on the brig *Alceste* bound for the Near East. He was accompanied by his wife and daughter and three friends. Perhaps he wished to duplicate the success of Chateaubriand's *Itinéraire de Paris à Jérusalem* and Hugo's *Orientales*. At any rate, an aspiring politician then could profit by a trip abroad even as he does today. During the voyage Julia, his daughter, died. At the same time, he received news of his election to the Chamber by the voters of Bergues.

The *Souvenirs, impressions, pensées, et paysages pendant un voyage en orient* was published in 1835 by Gosselin. In the final chapter Lamartine proposed a program to maintain peace in the Near East by a conference of the great powers. England, France, Austria, and Russia would establish a neutral zone there assuring mutual rights and Turkish sovereignty. There was a general fear even then of Russian intentions in the Mediterranean.

On the way to the Holy Land Lamartine stopped at Malta, Cyprus, and Greece. He reflected on the order and harmony of Greek architecture contrasted with the sorry state of Gothic cathedrals. The decline of European cathedrals symbolized to Lamartine the arrival of a new Christian era in which Christ's message took the form of a continuing revelation. Jesus' divinity was of little consequence. What did matter was the moral influence of Christianity. The poet foresaw a universal cult embracing all religions.

The conduct of Catholics in Palestine shocked Lamartine. Under the tolerant eyes of broad-minded Turks, slothful monks quarreled among themselves. If the situation were reversed, Lamartine doubted whether Christians would accord similar treatment to the Moslems.

In Syria he visited the eccentric and imperious Lady Hester Stanhope who through alleged powers of divination ruled the Druses of Mount Lebanon. There are colorful accounts of Maronite Christians, Bedouin tribes, and encounters with Arab chieftains. Lamartine's penchant for dramatizing events led him on one occasion to relate how he avoided a confrontation with a band of nomads.

The journey continued through Syria, Damascus, Balbec, Beirut, and Jaffa. At Constantinople Lamartine noted the Russian naval and military presence. He returned home through Bulgaria, Romania, Serbia, and Hungary.

Digressions characterized much of the *Voyage en orient*. There were copious quotations from Antar, the traditional poet-warrior of the Arabs. The itinerary was interspersed with observations on religion and politics as Lamartine made sweeping generalizations on the situation in the Near East and its implications for Europe. On the subject of religion Lamartine had his work placed on the Index when he predicted a universal cult in which the one true God would be honored in a diversity of social and linguistic patterns.

Remarks to the effect that truth was relative left little doubt about the persistence of the poet's eclectic frame of reference. Christianity seemed destined to undergo a process of purification and emerge stripped of dogmas and superstition. Truth had to be respected in all its forms, and one of the most important and ancient sources of religious inspiration now appeared to emanate from India, a follow-up of Lamartine's initial mention of Hinduism in the *Harmonies*.

An amusing sidelight of the *Voyage en orient* was the poet's visit to Lady Hester Stanhope. As Lamartine describes her, she was a figure from the *Arabian Nights* clad in the robes of an Arab seeress. Lamartine expounded to her his political and religious creed while in turn she discoursed on her own theology, a curious mixture of Islam, Judaism, and Christianity. The speech-making at an end, Lady Stanhope showed Lamartine the Arabian steed she kept for the coming of the second messiah.

Lamartine's account had obvious though significant discrepancies. He has Lady Stanhope address him as one of these "men of desire,"[4] a Martinist term for the privileged person endowed with insights into the divine plan. By no means an austere sorceress, in reality the blustery old English lady was incensed by the poet's affected manners and speech. Subsequent

visitors were subjected to her tantrums over the exaggerated
account in the *Voyage en orient*.

Even if Lamartine had been aware of Lady Stanhope's violent
reaction, he would have had little cause for concern. Successful sales of the *Voyage en orient* established his reputation as a
prose writer and widened his readership. This success coincided
with his emergence as a political figure, and the work was
frequently quoted in French, American, and English journals.

Although not considered today one of Lamartine's major works,
much of the *Voyage en orient* is written in a readable prose
style, and it is one of the better travel books of the period.
Fanciful as much of the description is, Lamartine did make on
the whole a sincere effort to understand different cultures in
the Near East. Many of the themes from the *Méditations* and
Harmonies reappear—broad speculations on political and social
issues, the progressive nature of revelation, and the sentimental
attachment to the memories of a childhood faith. Mention of
Hinduism and Martinism indicates these ideologies were not
erased from his mind. In short, when writing prose or poetry,
Lamartine's orientation remained basically unchanged.

VI Jocelyn

Jocelyn was published in 1836 by Gosselin and was intended
to be part of a longer epic never completed. At first glance,
it seemed logical that a presumably Catholic poet should write
about a priest, but the Vatican placed *Jocelyn* on the Index
along with the *Voyage en orient*. The poet suffered little remorse
from the decision and insisted many seminarians enjoyed
Jocelyn. He freely admitted Jocelyn was patterned after his
old friend the Abbé Dumont. Except for a romance before taking orders the worldly Dumont scarcely resembled Jocelyn.

Unperturbed by criticism, Lamartine outlined in the preface
his intention to show epic poetry could be both religious and
social in meaning. The complexity of modern society necessi-
tated, he insisted, a broader view of humanity. Poetry had
the advantage of raising a subject from the commonplace. In
selecting a current topic, Lamartine chose a priest to represent
one aspect of a complex society. In the poem Jocelyn is treated

as an average human being whose sacerdotal station is only incidental.

Jocelyn enters the seminary so his sister will have all the family's meager inheritance and a sufficient dowry. The revolution disrupts peaceful life at the seminary. Jocelyn takes refuge in the Alps and befriends a dying man who entrusts to him his son. The boy is in reality a beautiful girl, Laurence, in disguise. Jocelyn is summoned to prison by his bishop. The prelate faces execution and wants to ordain Jocelyn in order to have a priest present to administer the Last Sacrament. Torn between duty and love for Laurence, Jocelyn, nevertheless, submits. Laurence departs grief-stricken on learning about his ordination. As pastor in an Alpine village Jocelyn teaches his flock tolerance and an undogmatic religion. On a trip to Paris he sees Laurence, now a public sinner. Some time later he is called to the bedside of a dying woman whom he recognizes as Laurence. She is buried next to her father. Soon afterward Jocelyn dies, and the two lovers are reunited in death.

Throughout the poem Jocelyn's uncertainty about his decision to be a priest is manifest. He finds momentary happiness with Laurence. She experiences a spiritual ecstasy as they both view the awesome panorama spread before them:

Ah! if it is so, sweet breezes of the dawn, carry us away with the fragrance of the flowers. Take us where souls are united! We will pray better to the God adored by the star. . . .[5]

When their idyl is broken by the bishop's message, a Cornelian conflict of love and duty ensues. The enraged prelate, a latter-day Horace, excoriates Jocelyn for yielding to an earthly affection: "You are no longer a Christian or priest of Jesus. Get out of my sight . . . I no longer know you!"[6] Thoroughly browbeaten, a bewildered Jocelyn submits to the ordination. This portion of the narrative dismayed Protestant and Catholic critics with its errors and inaccuracies, but the average reader did not question Lamartine's orthodoxy. No bishop of course could have conferred orders under such conditions to an unwilling candidate simply to obtain a priest to administer the Last Sacrament. Lamartine is at least consistent in having Jocelyn, once ordained, act as an atypical priest for nineteenth-century France. When villagers refuse to bury a dead Jew they become the object of a severe pastoral tongue-lashing. Since the older villagers are beyond hope, Jocelyn tries to teach greater tolerance to the younger generation:

I do not overload their senses and their mind with a sterile learning nourished by pride. I instruct their conscience rather than their reason. Nature and their eyes that's my whole technique![7]

Rousseau's approach to religion is evident in these lines. Another non-Catholic view may be perceived in Jocelyn's explanation to the village children of the divine principle underlying nature: "It is this immense, infinite, immortal soul which sees more than the star and will outlive it!"[8] There is a touch of Hinduism to this picture of the divinity, a repetition of an earlier description in the *Harmonies*. The poet thereby laid himself open to charges of pantheism, an accusation he always denied. For him it was merely an appropriate image to emphasize the unity of the world. Reference is made to Christianity and its founder as well. When the poet does so, he pictures Jocelyn comparing his sufferings with those of Jesus: "O Christ! like you I have sweated out my agony in these three double nights of horror and sleeplessness!"[9]

Association of personal trials and tribulations with those Christ experienced was a trait common to Romantic poets, and Lamartine was no exception. To accusations of undue self-pity on Jocelyn's part the poet would have replied that his priest was an ordinary human, not a saintly ascetic. Other scenes in the poem—the death of Jocelyn's mother and Laurence—recall the sentimentalism of "Le Crucifix" and convinced devout readers of the poet's orthodoxy. The skeptical did not have far to look to find evidence of a changed attitude toward the Church. An ardent Catholic of the time would not decry the moment "when these fishermen leaving the evangelical bark cast upon the world their political net...."[10]

Definitely involved in politics by now, Lamartine already felt the pressure of anticlericals about him in the Chamber.

One section of the poem, "Les Laboureurs" is more in keeping with the poetic powers previously displayed in the *Méditations* and *Harmonies*. Jocelyn contemplates a pastoral setting and recalls happier days with Laurence:

The earth which breaks under the ploughshare that (in turn) it sharpens, piles up and breaks into quivering pieces and on being exposed (to the air) vaporizes like a piece of flesh which splits and throbs and steams under the iron.[11]

Such lines constitute the main redeeming feature of *Jocelyn,* otherwise a mediocre tale in verse. "Les Laboureurs" compares favorably with the better lyrics of Lamartine but is not sufficient to compensate entirely for the poem's defects. In itself the plot is a rehash of the worst Romantic clichés, and Lamartine's narrative style in poetry quickly becomes wearisome.

Perhaps *Jocelyn's* greatest value is in being a document of the poet's literary, political, and philosophical aspirations at a crucial stage in his career. It was also one of the significant attempts at epic poetry in the nineteenth century. Since the Renaissance, many French writers had tried to produce a successful epic poem. Lamartine's effort received considerable recognition, although Hugo was to outstrip him with *La Légende des siècles*. Political implications of *Jocelyn* were obvious in the liberal religion it preached and in its interpretation of the priest's role in modern society. The poet's theology reconfirmed the views already expressed in the *Harmonies*. God as depicted by Lamartine had Hinduistic facets, and humanity had to measure the quality of religious principles by their relevance to current moral and social needs. *Jocelyn* marked another step forward in the poet's philosophical and political outlook but a relapse in the quality of his literary production.

VII   La Chute d'un ange

La Chute d'un ange was published in 1838 by Gosselin. Lamartine's second narrative poem was also to be a part of a longer epic, along with *Jocelyn,* tracing the successive stages of human development as man realized his divine destiny. Cédar, the main character, was an angel who fell into sin and was obliged to live among mortals. As with *Jocelyn*, Lamartine denied any intent to attack Christianity, which of the various revelations made by God he still considered the most perfect and sublime. An angel, Cédar, falls in love with a mortal, the comely Daïdha. The story takes place in Asia Minor in biblical times. For his sin he is condemned to assume human form. Cédar has two children by Daïdha, who is buried alive with them in punishment for her fornication. They are rescued by Cédar, and all flee into the desert. There they meet the wise man, Adonaï, who teaches them the true will of God. Soldiers of the wicked Nemphed kill Adonaï, seize Cédar and his family, and transport them to the tyrant's palace in a flying machine. Nemphed is assassinated and replaced by the equally villainous Arasfiel. One of the royal concubines, Lakmi, seduces Cédar by trickery. Enraged, Cédar hurls Lakmi into a chasm and kills Arasfiel. After fleeing into the wilderness, Cédar and his family are abandoned by their guide. Daïdha and the children die, and Cédar casts himself upon a funeral pyre erected for them.

Lamartine entitled the chapters "Visions" to emphasize the prophetic character of the poem. The language at times retains much of the rhythm of liturgical prayers in Latin whenever Lamartine describes a moment of meditation. A case in point is Adonaï's paraphrase of the Lord's Prayer:

O Father of every creature, he said, whose temple is everywhere where nature extends, whose presence hollows out and fills infinity, may your name be blessed everywhere in every soul.[12]

While prayerful moments do occur in *La Chute d'un ange*, Lamartine also treated a more mundane theme, the virginal beauty of Daïdha that caught Cédar's eye:

Her hair, stirred by the light evening breeze, waved on her arms like a large black veil, allowing to shine forth her white shoulders, or the roundness of her bosom, or the contours of her hips.[13]

The description of the thirteen-year-old Daïdha, a Romantic nymphet, angered prudish critics. Possibly Lamartine was thinking of Shakespeare's Juliet when he made Daïdha the same age. The sculptural quality of the word pictures shows again

Lamartine's partial affinity to the Parnassians and admiration of Classical lines in the plastic arts.

Lamartine adds a touch of science fiction and anticipates Jules Verne by almost two decades when Cédar suddenly espies a primitive airplane: "A celestial ship, strange in form, covering with its broad wingspread a patch of air."[14]

Much of the story line savors of French Romantic melodrama, with all the familiar stereotypes, commonplaces, and claptrap. Cédar, the hero, is fittingly handsome and courageous, and Daïdha, the heroine, is appropriately attractive and defenseless. There are villains galore and a sufficient number of action-packed episodes to furnish material for a novel. Lakmi's ruse to trap Cédar in bed by posing as Daïdha would seem to satisfy any demands for sexuality. In fact, Lamartine's preoccupation here with feminine pulchritude and risqué situations has been traced to the Marquis de Sade, whom the poet probably read on the sly when an inquisitive adolescent.

Lamartine was foxy enough to see the value of melodramatic episodes in promoting popular sales. In his own comments on the poem he emphasized its philosophical significance. Fashionable critics did pounce upon the work's moral and religious implications. More often than not, the "Fragment of the Primitive Book" in the Eighth Vision was the special target of their attack. In this section Adonaï, the old prophet, preaches to Cédar and Daïdha on God's message to mankind. Although he has a book supposedly containing eternal verities Adonaï tells the young couple one book with unprinted pages surpasses all others:

The only divine book in which He writes His name constantly growing [in magnitude], man, is your spirit! It's your reason, mirror of the supreme reason where some shadow of Himself is painted in your darkness.[15]

More so than in previous works, Saint-Martin makes his presence felt in La Chute d'un ange. Man as the divine book of God's revelation is a Martinist image. The most apparent direct borrowing from Saint-Martin is in the title of the Eighth Vision. "Primitive Book" was used by Saint-Martin to describe the "man of desire" as the repository of celestial revelation in human society. In the "Fragment of the Primitive Book" the concept of direct revelation is discussed along with other Martinist notions—man's need to pass through a period of expiation and a forecast of a millennium.

Hinduism is less in evidence, although Lamartine does slip momentarily into pantheism when Adonaï depicts the divine essence

Where the whole is part and the part complete, where life and death, time and matter are nothing more in effect than forms of the mind, mysterious circles that describe everything in Him....[16]

The poet usually tried to sidestep charges of pantheism by saying his interests were not those of the professional philosopher when it was quite apparent he liked to toy with philosophical concepts as much as with political principles. Central to Lamartine's belief in the necessity of a sound social order was the idea that the moral drive in man was intuitive, a notion expounded by Adonaï:

The social code destined to increase, has in our nature an innate basis, this ineffable instinct of supreme justice which in us protests in secret against ourselves.[17]

Adonaï extends this principle on a broader scale to apply to nations and to international justice. Unquestionably, Lamartine was affected in part by Saint-Simon and Fourier with their dreams of universal peace and harmony. Theosophists also foresaw a millennium when peace and order would prevail. Of immediate concern to the poet-politician was disseminating in his writings the policy of international peace mentioned in his speeches in the Chamber of Deputies.

Readers today are primarily interested in *La Chute d'un ange* as a documentation of Lamartine's literary and religious thinking in the 1830's. Few would agree with Edgar Allan Poe that it is one of the poet's best efforts. Lamartine's idea of epic grandeur is nothing more than the usual commonplaces of Romantic melodrama with one emotional episode following another. Incidental passages from the "Fragment of the Primitive Book" are vaguely reminiscent of clearer and sharper lines on philosophical questions in the poetry of Voltaire. By comparison, *Jocelyn* has a lyric charm that rescues it from the mediocrity of *La Chute d'un ange.*

If Lamartine's announcement of a new era of poetry in the "Destinées de la poésie" is to be taken seriously, then *La Chute d'un ange* can scarcely be called a glorious fulfillment of that prophecy. A random selection of one of his political talks would provide a better sample of the literary quality he could impart to a social message on the human condition. Many critics conclude with regret that *La Chute d'un ange* only proves that Lamartine's true talent was in the lyric. There his Eclecticism, with its allusion to Martinism and Hinduism, found a more charming and delicate expression.

VIII   Recueillements poétiques

The *Recueillements poétiques* was published in 1839 by Gosselin and represented Lamartine's last significant volume of poetry. Henceforth, except for an occasional poem, he would devote his time to politics and to prose works.

In the main, the poems in the collection are patterned along the same lines as the *Méditations* and *Harmonies.* As on other occasions, he is unable to resist momentarily the rather pantheistic thought of becoming one with the Creator:

Then my soul, having been merged into the great oneness, dissolved, a weak drop lost in the bosom of the seas, an insensitive load tossed by the Ocean; but where the serene or convulsive impulse which from the total abyss travels from wave to wave, throbs in the drop of water. (A. M. Felix Guillemardet)[18]

In the foregoing, the effect of Lamartine's probable reading of Guigniaut-Creuzer is in evidence. Hindu genesis represented water as the primitive element from which the deity arose and into which individual souls were eventually reabsorbed.

In "Utopie," a focal point of the *Recueillements,* Lamartine envisions the future when denominational barriers will be leveled:

A single cult links the world, animated by a single love. Its dogma, where enlightenment abounds, is only one Gospel in broad daylight.[19]

This dream of a universal religion is the central theme of "Utopie" in its reminder to mankind that revelation comes directly to man and is a continuing process. People must discard the superstitions of the past and, in the new universal cult based on love, heed the message of Christ without the distortions added by human interpretation:

It is the pure word of Calvary, not like the one from which, in earthly tones, the distant echo of the sanctuary allowed the divine meaning to escape. . . .[20]

"Utopie" is probably the best and most meaningful poem of the *Recueillements,* recapitulating and enlarging upon one of the principal motifs of the *Harmonies;* Christianity is the key to human progress, but man must grasp the essence of its teaching in Christ's suffering and moral example. While Lamartine identified himself with Christ like Vigny and other Romantic poets he saw in Jesus' life reason for optimism, not stoical resignation. In "Utopie" Lamartine incorporates some of his best techniques in a prayerlike style to relate man's religious quest and future prospects.

What baffled listeners to his political speeches becomes clearer in his poetry where he unfolds his vision of what is in store for mankind. United by love, nations will abandon international conflict. Religious disputes will cease through the establishment of a universal cult. This latter idea smacks of Saint-Simonism, but it was also a Martinist teaching. In all probability, Lamartine envisaged a society led by the poet-theosophist, the "man of desire." That assignment, he hoped, would be his in France.

The *Recueillements* has often been found disappointing after the *Harmonies.* Much of this criticism is unjustified. Although the poems are fewer in number, they still show his lyrical powers were not on the decline. Much of the old religious feeling and social consciousness is still expressed with the same rhythmic flow of which he was past master.

IX   Histoire des Girondins

The *Histoire des Girondins* was published in eight volumes in 1847 by Furne. Understandably, it caused a furore as the work of a prominent literary and political figure. The July Monarchy was already toppling, and the *Histoire des Girondins* helped to hasten its overthrow. During the composition of the history Lamartine made few appearances in the Chamber. With its publication, Lamartine acquired a reputation for liberalism and broadened his voter appeal. Interest in France was both political and literary. There was general approval of Lamartine's style but much criticism of inaccuracies in historical interpretation. The most curious readers were students of the political scene, but they had difficulty in pinpointing the exact position of the poet-politician. While commending the underlying principles of the revolution, Lamartine deplored its attendant bloodshed. Louis XVI, a symbol of basic faults of the monarchy, appeared to be an innocent bystander. With the variety of opinions inserted by Lamartine, readers could choose their own interpretation according to their convictions—Monarchist, Republican, or Socialist.

Lamartine starts with a description of the state of affairs in 1791 and brief analyses of leading figures in the drama. The revolution was at the crossroads, and political societies and newspapers were being founded everywhere. Louis XVI's abortive attempt to escape aroused antiroyalist sentiment. Party lines were formed on the question of how to punish the king. As the Assembly vacillated, the mob clamored for the king's head and the overthrow of the republic. By prompt action Lafayette restrained the people, but considerable tension remained. A new constitution was drawn up which the king accepted.

Meanwhile, the crowned heads of Europe mobilized against revolutionary France. Hurriedly, plans for national defense were discussed at Paris. Threatened by invasion and internal dissension, the Republic seemed ready to crumble any minute. For the moment Danton was emerging as temporary head all the while Madame Roland encouraged Girondist intrigue and Robespierre curried favor with the Jacobins.

The Duke of Brunswick's manifesto revived the people's fighting spirit. Instead of halting mob violence, Danton and Marat took steps to increase it. According to Lamartine, Danton assumed responsibility for the September Massacre of innocent persons. Quarrels broke out between Jacobins and Girondists over the king's fate and ended in the unhappy monarch's death. Europe reacted in anger. General Dumouriez triumphed on the battlefield and then turned traitor. As rival factions accused each other of disloyalty, political leaders were struck down one by one. Marat won out over the Girondists only to be assassinated by Charlotte Corday. With him out of the way, Danton and Robespierre vied for leadership.

Today's executioner was tomorrow's victim in the ruthless power struggle. The cruel and impersonal guillotine numbered Madame Roland among its victims. Danton and Robespierre joined forces to remove Hébert, who set up the machinery for the Terror, and then they turned against each other. Time was running out for Danton; arrested with Desmoulins on charges of corruption, he was tried and executed.

Under Robespierre the Terror continued unabated and claimed illustrious victims like André Chénier. Once in command, Robespierre experienced all the frustrations of his predecessors. Despite a vicious and cunning battle to stay in power, Robespierre succumbed to hard times and persistent political opposition. Thus ended five years of the Revolution which to many seemed like five centuries.

Today nobody takes seriously Lamartine's evaluation of the Revolution. To be appreciated, the work must be approached as an imaginative piece of prose fiction. It is a lengthy series of vignettes interspersed with animated descriptions of conspiracies, battles, and stormy sessions in the Assembly. Much of the book resembles a movie scenario with closeups juxtaposed with views of large crowds. The narration is episodic, and there is a constant shifting of scenes as though Lamartine were striving for visual effects. Whether or not the recent development of photography had an unconscious effect on him can only be conjectured.

From the first volume Lamartine prepared readers for a well-paced narrative and presented one of the many portraits for

which the history became famous. Mirabeau is analyzed as one
who dominated contemporaries by astuteness, not by virtue. In
the careful weighing and balancing of terms that typifies so
often the style of Lamartine in this instance, the hand of La
Rochefoucauld or La Bruyère can be detected. The Romantic
poet turned prosateur read the seventeenth-century stylists with
profit.

The portrait of Danton aroused discussion among antirepub-
licans even though Lamartine recognized in him the Machia-
vellian intention to use the Revolution as a means to seize power.
An unprincipled demagogue, Danton could control a mob with
ease. In some ways he resembled Lamartine. Both came from
families of average means in the provinces and received a solid,
basic education at home before going to school where alert
minds enabled them to succeed with minimal effort. With
Danton's death the Revolution lost a certain dash and *éclat*.

Lamartine's sketch of Robespierre brought further criticism.
Unlike Danton, Lamartine considered Robespierre a sincere
supporter of the Revolution who unfortunately deemed himself
the only person capable of passing judgment on a man's loyalty
to the cause. Whereas Danton made violence a means to achieve
power, Robespierre felt it a necessary evil to produce an ultimately ideal social order.

Marat represented still another paradox. He worked for the
abolition of capital punishment but had no compunction about
mass murder. His aim was not a simple reform of the existing
government but a complete overthrow of the establishment.
Charlotte Corday cut short any hopes of accomplishing that
objective. Nurtured on the writings of Rousseau and Plutarch's
works, Charlotte Corday was not a person to be suspected of
contemplating assassination. Yet she had Joan of Arc's burning
love of country and visions of a mission to save France, an
obsession that led to self-immolation. The vignette of Charlotte
Corday became a favorite of readers and one of the most frequently published excerpts from the *Histoire des Girondins*. In
the United States it was dramatized on the stage.

Charlotte's sacrifice was foreign to Madame Roland's nature.
All through her trial and imprisonment she made herself the

center of attention. Totally irreligious, only the approval of her peers and that of posterity mattered to her. Lamartine did acknowledge at least her stoical resignation when she saw Robespierre, fearful of the Convention, would not intercede. More pathetic was Marie Antoinette. Lamartine judged her at the end almost unaware of her former rank and bereaved by the murder of her husband and the disappearance of her son.

Bourbonist sympathies may have inspired the gentle treatment of Marie Antoinette and Louis XVI, a victim of circumstances and not an enemy of liberty. Lamartine tried to show how the king wished to forestall the Revolution by not being too autocratic and was guilty of poor decisions, not of evil intentions. The people and their leaders were also to blame. Since the king's death destroyed the original idealism of 1789, Lamartine questioned the morality of any revolution that resorted to murder.

With a penchant for contrasts, Lamartine drew a vivid word portrait of Louis-Philippe's father, dubbed Philippe Egalité by the Convention. Louis XVI was willing to accept the Duc d'Orléans' bid for reconciliation, but the king's household insulted the renegade aristocrat. The infuriated outcast cooperated with the Girondists and voted for the execution of Louis XVI.

Lamartine's contrast of the royal martyr and his Judas served a political purpose. Legitimists appreciated the none-too-subtle reminder of Orleanist treachery. The writer-politician was seeking support from all quarters. Republican and Socialist factions responded favorably to praise of Voltaire and Rousseau. The Vicaire Savoyard cognizant of God's hand in the universe dreamed of a utopian social order, which, if impractical, at least pointed the way to a better life.

The sharp, satirical pen of Voltaire was a far cry from the visionary Rousseau. Lamartine acknowledged Voltaire's brilliance and crusade in the cause of tolerance but deplored the great *philosophe's* antireligious diatribes. The cold view of a remote deity repelled the author, who regretted Voltaire's unequivocal rejection of all belief in the supernatural.

It was Lamartine's conviction that the ideals of Christianity and rationalism were compatible. Scholars today also find a

common ground for the principles of the French Revolution
and those of Christ. In keeping with his eclectic approach to
religion and politics, the poet sought to harmonize both schools
of thought. One could not exist without the other, for true
progress required retaining values proven necessary to man by
past experience. He was too convinced of Christianity's moral
contributions to envisage France without the Church in some
form. Plans to modernize and reform Catholicism met with his
approval, but he did not favor a frigid Voltairean cult to replace
all belief in the supernatural. Praise of Voltaire in the *Histoire
des Girondins* applied only to the distinguished philosopher's
crusade for social justice. An understanding of this point is
essential to a proper evaluation of *Le Désert*, to be discussed
in a subsequent chapter.

X *Evaluation*

The *Histoire des Girondins* is Lamartine's most significant
prose work. Only when judged as a piece of creative writing
can it be fully appreciated. Among the French Romantics history
was, for all practical purposes, a specific genre and embodied
one of that movement's main objectives—the re-creation of the
past. Lamartine accomplishes that very objective by re-creating
in colorful and striking terms the rise and fall of the Girondists.
Its most noteworthy feature is the vivid series of vignettes of
leading figures of the period. Preoccupation on Lamartine's
part with an analysis of their motives in a frequently epi-
grammatic style brings to mind the Classical writers and their
probing of the motives that actuate men. Like them, Lamartine
investigates the general causes of human acts as exemplified
by the Revolution. In some respects the *Histoire des Girondins*
has borrowings from the Romantic novel and theater. The subject is drawn from French history with a number of subplots
related to the central one on the actions resulting from the
Terror. Many individual scenes, charged with the emotion and
tension of a French melodrama, could easily be staged.

Chief among the work's drawbacks are repetition, its length,
and the insertion of some episodes, such as those concerning
Vergniaud and unrelated events outside Paris, that detract from

the development of the main narrative. Professional historians take seriously few of Lamartine's interpretations. From a historical standpoint, the *Histoire des Girondins* has value only as a reflection of the poet-politician's thinking in relation to the events of 1848. In this respect, he does not appear the bungler he is often made out to be. If not the most astute student of politics, he did realize some of the basic principles of campaigning by not openly declaring his candidacy as Louis-Philippe's successor. Aware that his power base lay in conservative and moderate elements, he did not make the *Histoire des Girondins* an incendiary and revolutionary tract addressed solely to the urban proletariat. Instead he sought a broader audience and coyly reminded readers of the traitorous conduct of Louis-Philippe's father who joined the radicals and voted for Louis XVI's execution. Sales of the work and Lamartine's initial popularity in 1848 attest to the success of his strategy.

With the *Histoire des Girondins* Lamartine took his place among the better prose writers of French Romanticism. A flexible and clear style linked him with the tradition established by Classical prosateurs, and a lively reconstruction of the past made him a creditable representative of those French Romantics for whom history was a distinct literary genre.

XI   Trois Mois au pouvoir

Trois Mois au pouvoir was published in 1848 by Lévy and covers the period when Lamartine was head of the provisional government. Disavowing any collusion with extremists, Lamartine tells how he sought peaceful reform. Revolution had to be accomplished through the force of ideas. He talks of a new, liberal form of Christianity. His refusal to disband the troops in Paris, he insists, helped to insure law and order. In excerpts from his speeches Lamartine shows how he refused to intervene in Poland or Italy and addressed divergent groups composed of students, soldiers, workers, fishermen, and Freemasons.

Lamartine irritated contemporaries by living in the past. While the work has some value as a document of the times, actual events are obscured by Lamartine's urge to play the demigod. Undoubtedly his words affected listeners in 1848, but the author seems to forget the memory of man is unreliable. His defeat in the presidential race should have taught him that much.

XII   Histoire de la Révolution de 1848

The *Histoire de la Révolution de 1848* was published in 1849 by Perrotin in Paris in two volumes. Reaction to the work varied according to the attitude of the individual reviewer toward Lamartine. While the work did not create the same furore as the *Histoire des Girondins,* the poet-statesman was still fresh in people's minds, and many were interested in his personal assessment of the events of 1848.

Whatever the results may have been, Lamartine credits the Revolution of 1848 with initially good motives. He freely discusses the good and bad points of contemporaries. Louis-Philippe, while well intentioned, did not maintain a steady program of social reform. Although guilty of political blunders, Louis Blanc insisted on a policy of peaceful change. Only the revolutionaries, led by Barbès and Raspail, deliberately promoted violence.

On the diplomatic front Lamartine prides himself on a very successful effort. Reassurances to England and a hands-off policy in Poland and Italy that mollified Russia and Austria kept peace in Europe. At home, he maintains, violence was temporarily averted, although Cavaignac and he disagreed on advance preparations to forestall a workers' revolt in Paris.

In the area of domestic priorities Lamartine insists on the need at the time for separation of Church and state with proper safeguards for freedom of religion. Of equal importance was the need to eliminate glaring inequities in civil and economic rights of the common man. Lamartine's hope of rectifying abuses vanished with his loss of power.

By writing a history of his own exploits in the third person, Lamartine did not endear himself to contemporaries. Rambling excerpts from political speeches would have us believe he left many an audience spellbound. Equally annoying are Lamartine's sly references to his bravery and accomplishments in 1848, all made with a thinly veiled self-esteem.

On the positive side of the ledger, the *Histoire de la Révolution de 1848* has its merits. Louis-Philippe is not the leading villain of the drama, nor are the Socialists directly blamed for popular violence. Only the openly terrorist groups are singled out for criticism. Leftist historians would undoubtedly disagree and point out that conservative financiers did as much if not more to undermine the Second Republic.

Isolated incidents are vividly described: the rejection of the Duchesse d'Orléans' bid for a regency, the selection of the tricolor over the red flag of communism, and the abdication of Louis-Philippe. Unlike the *Histoire des Girondins*, there are few vignettes. Lamartine's ingratiating prose style saves the *Histoire de la Révolution de 1848* more than once from being a monotonous recitation of the facts. Still, it is evident that Lamartine's ability to write history as a literary genre was limited. He had already reached his peak in the *Histoire des Girondins* where he reconstructed the past with some depth of feeling, but he could not do this indefinitely in a long series of involved histories. This shortcoming was to prove his undoing in subsequent attempts at historical writing.

XIII Confidences

The *Confidences,* including the tale *Graziella,* was published in 1849 by Perrotin. The series of reminiscences about Lamartine's childhood and adolescence had been in preparation for several years. Disclosure of intimate details of his private life invited enemies of the writer to subject him to public ridicule. By his own admission, the facts were embellished to make the book more attractive to readers.

The first pages of the *Confidences* relate how Lamartine's parents met and the hardships of the Revolution when his father was temporarily imprisoned. He pictures himself being reared in two traditions, the sentimental Catholicism of his mother and the Voltairean rationalism of his father. Allowed to roam about the countryside and play with the farmers' children, he also had the benefit of hearing his parents read aloud in the evening from great works of literature. Dissatisfied with the first boarding school to which he was sent, Lamartine enrolled at

Belley and profited by his studies there and by the lasting friendships he formed.

His sojourn in Italy is related in *Graziella*. Fleeing to Switzerland during the Hundred Days, he tells of seeing Madame de Staël and other celebrities, the most intriguing being the formidable apologist of the papacy, Joseph de Maistre. Of an entirely different disposition was the worldly Abbé Dumont who lived near Mâcon. A priest who went hunting more often than he said mass, the Abbé Dumont according to gossip in the area originally entered the seminary owing to an unhappy love affair.

It is just as easy today to size up the *Confidences* for what they are, a novelistic version of Lamartine's life with all the defects and outlandish details of *Raphaël*. Contemporaries deemed his revelations in poor taste and ludicrous. A fluent prose style did not overcome the work's many drawbacks. Lamartine seemingly was unaware of the extent to which his egotism aggravated readers.

In such a book there is necessarily much of interest to researchers. Details on Joseph de Maistre are of value especially since the Catholic apologist also admired Saint-Martin and was thus a potential source of information for Lamartine on the theosophist. The section on Abbé Dumont also shows how the unorthodox pastor served as a model for Jocelyn. While a fair portion of Lamartine's statements seems substantiated by the facts, much of the narration is fanciful and of doubtful veracity.

XIV   Graziella

Graziella, first published with the *Confidences* in 1849, was subsequently published as a separate edition. Based on a love affair with a Neapolitan girl during his stay in Italy in the 1800's, *Graziella* was one of the most popular of the works written by Lamartine after 1848.

On a visit to Italy with a friend, Virieu, Lamartine meets Graziella who with her two small brothers lives with their grandparents in a fishing village. The two young Frenchmen take up the fisherfolk's way of life. Graziella is unimpressed by Lamartine's conversation about Latin and Italian writers but becomes enthusiastic upon hearing the story of *Paul et Virginie.* She nurses Lamartine back to health when he falls ill. Faced with the prospect of marrying one of the boys from the village, she realizes, as does Lamartine, that they love each other. Summoned home for a time, Lamartine learns of Graziella's death during his absence and receives her last letter. Later he sees in a church the body of a young girl who reminds him of Graziella.

The original Graziella, a Neapolitan cigar-maker, had quite a passionate affair with Lamartine in 1811. Although she came from a fishing village, she was not the sweet innocent girl of Lamartine's romance but a seductive wench. After his involvement with her the writer wanted to end the affair. Only later did he romanticize the liaison in Naples.

It is needless to point out the patent defects of *Graziella*— the maudlin love story, improbable characterizations, and monotonous dialogue. The tale has nonetheless a few attractive aspects. In the family of Andréa, the old fisherman, Lamartine captures some of the simple, kindly spirit of the common people and grasps some of the basic elements of local color. There is a pathetic charm in Graziella's efforts to please the young Frenchman. Descriptions of the sea and countryside are another of the book's merits. Despite these redeeming features, *Graziella* remains a saccharine yarn. Its appeal to contemporaries is surprising. Flaubert, no great admirer of Lamartine, was obliged to admit his fondness for *Graziella.*

XV Raphaël

Raphaël was published in 1849 by Perrotin. Readers of course instantly recognized it as an account of Lamartine's love affair with Julie Charles. The fact of the poet-statesman's political defeat only encouraged hostile critics to assail the work's overdrawn sentimentality.

As Raphaël, Lamartine relates his romance with Julie Charles. While staying at a resort in Savoy, Raphaël rescues Julie when her boat capsizes. Their friendship blossoms into love although their relationship remains platonic. At loggerheads on the subject of religion, in which Raphaël's theism clashes with Julie's agnos-

ticism, they enjoy the same literary tastes in their admiration
of Goethe and Bernardin de Saint-Pierre. Julie's health worsens
and she leaves the resort. Later they are reunited in Paris
where Lamartine meets Julie's husband, a famous scientist. The
two lovers plan to meet again at the resort, but Raphaël goes
there to receive word of her death. Heartbroken, Raphaël
is consoled by the thought of Julie's conversion to Christianity
and the promise of their eventual reunion in heaven.

From the outset Lamartine creates a bad impression in
Raphaël. Reference in the preface to the hero's physical perfection amounts to self-adoration. It is readily understandable
why the book provoked laughter in sophisticated circles. Occasional passages of pretty prose brightened an otherwise dull
and repetitious narrative. Readers had taken the same trip in
the *Méditations,* so the scenery was familiar. Boat-rowing with
Julie on the lake was a reprise of "Le Lac." Communion with
nature and human love as a reflection of divine love were by
now overworked themes.

Raphaël at least throws some light on Lamartine's concept
of the novel, an outdated one in the mid-nineteenth century.
A pale imitation of *La Nouvelle Héloïse, Raphaël* repeats only
the platonic phase of the relationship between Rousseau's two
lovers. George Sand used with greater success the theme of
idealized love, while Lamartine had only an elementary grasp
of the workings of the human mind. Raphaël and Julie repeatedly
wail about their sad destiny, with no other motivation to explain
their acts. Apparently Lamartine thought the novel had pro-
gressed little since 1800. *Raphaël* has all the drawbacks of the
sentimental novels of Constant and Madame de Staël with none
of their fine delineation of character. Oddly enough, Lamartine's
attempt at writing a history of the Girondists resulted in a
fairly good historical novel.

CHAPTER 4

Period of Decline

I Toussaint L'Ouverture

TOUSSAINT L'OUVERTURE was published in 1850 by Michel-Lévy. It had been composed in 1840, and for a time the manuscript was lost. When asked by Michel-Lévy in 1848 whether he had a text ready for the press, Lamartine sent the publisher *Toussaint L'Ouverture.* Subsequently the play was performed at the Theatre of Porte Saint-Martin on April 6, 1850, with the popular Frédérick Lemaître in the title role. The play received some praise, but the reaction of the audience was negative. Since Lamartine always espoused abolition and finally freed slaves on French soil in 1848, the subject was a logical one for him to treat.

Toussaint, the Haitian leader, is troubled by the arrival of French forces. His nephew, Moïse, suspects him of planning to be dictator. Disguised as a blind man and accompanied by his niece, Adrienne, Toussaint penetrates the French lines. There he sees his two sons, Isaac and Albert, sent back to Haiti to persuade their father to cooperate with Napoleon. Albert idolizes Bonaparte, while Isaac leans toward the Haitian cause. French soldiers attack Toussaint but are restrained by the wife of General Leclerc. The general, not recognizing Toussaint, asks him to bear a message of amnesty to the Haitian forces. When Moïse appears to join the French, Toussaint kills the traitor and escapes. Adrienne, however, is captured. Isaac and Albert try to help her escape but are prevented by Salvador, their tutor, who soon discovers the girl is his own daughter. At Salvador's request a priest takes Adrienne back to Toussaint. Isaac and Albert come to their father as hostages of the French to ask him to surrender. Isaac remains with Toussaint, but Albert returns to the French. Adrienne holds aloft the Haitian banner and is killed by a fusillade. Enraged, Toussaint sounds the call to arms as the play ends.

Lamartine takes considerable liberty with historical facts. The real Toussaint was a capable leader but was not above switching allegiance at various times for personal gain. He at first acquiesced to Leclerc before plotting the revolt that led to his imprisonment and death. His sons, sent to Haiti to ask him to side with Napoleon, died in obscurity in France. Salvador and Adrienne are fictitious characters.

The play itself is an unintentional satire on the worst features of Romantic melodrama. Characters mouth singsong lines. Toussaint is more of a caricature than a characterization and lacks a consistent motivation. The subplot of Adrienne and Salvador disintegrates in midair.

Perhaps the only parts of the drama meaningful to contemporary readers are those concerned with black identity. At the opening of the play there is a black version of the "Marseillaise." When Isaac reproaches Albert for collaborating with the whites he stresses loyalty to one's cultural and racial origins.

If the experience with *Saül* did not persuade Lamartine to put aside thoughts of a career as playwright, the failure of *Toussaint L'Ouverture* certainly convinced him once and for all. Today the drama is a museum piece of interest to specialists alone and a sad reminder of a low point in Lamartine's later literary production.

II   Geneviève

Geneviève, histoire d'une servante, was published in 1850 by Chaix. Like the *Tailleur de pierres de Saint-Point,* it dealt with the suffering of poor people.

Geneviève, servant of the unfortunate Jocelyn, tells Lamartine of her trials and tribulations. At the beginning of the story she is unable to marry Cyprien because of the task of rearing her sister, Josette. When Josette dies after having a baby by a soldier, Septième, a kindly nurse who cares for the child, is accused of kidnapping. To save the nurse, Mère Belan, Geneviève claims the infant as her own but loses it to an orphanage. Later Geneviève meets Cyprien and Mère Belan who exonerates

her. A plague strikes down Cyprien and his family, and Geneviève finds a new home with a young couple, Jean and Luce.
Unknown to Jean, Luce adopted another baby when their own
was killed. Geneviève discovers the adopted child is Josette's. A
relative of Septième allows Geneviève and the young couple to
keep the child and provides for it with an income from Septième's
will.

With *Geneviève* Lamartine attempts to write a social novel.
Consequently it has more elements of realism than his other
writings. Geneviève's story, although a little exaggerated, does
represent many of the injustices experienced by the lower classes.
Miserable conditions in orphanages and prisons are depicted with
some accuracy. Lamartine himself had deep compassion for
abandoned children. Much of the novel, however, relies on
coincidence, and the dialogue shows no feeling for the language and idiom of the proletariat. As in *Graziella*, Lamartine
does recognize considerable virtue in the common people. *Geneviève* has the same moralizing about the poor typical of George
Sand, but Lamartine lacks her ability to arrive at basic psychological insights. With all its shortcomings nonetheless *Geneviève* is a welcome relief from the tiresome emotionalism of
Raphaël.

III   Le Conseiller du peuple

Le Conseiller du peuple was published in periodical form from
1849 to 1851 by Lamartine. As self-appointed adviser to the
people, he commented on the civic duties of persons in various
walks of life and of the family and the state as well. The publication was successful since Lamartine had not lost all his following after being defeated at the polls. With Louis Napoleon's
coup d'état, *Le Conseiller du peuple* ceased publication.

Numerous excerpts from Lamartine's old political speeches
fill many a page. As before, he warned French voters about a
variety of threats—socialism, the Orleanists, and the need to
preserve religious values. Church and state had to be separated,
but freedom of religion was a necessary guarantee of a moral
order. Equally important was a free press that did not distort
the news. In the Chamber deputies had to voice the wishes

of their constituency to help the government of Louis Napoleon succeed in its task. Lamartine felt it best to credit the new president with good intentions and discounted rumors of an impending coup d'état. Only at the end of the *Conseiller* was he obliged to admit a mistake in judgment.

The *Conseiller du peuple* is an indication of Lamartine's political thinking in the period immediately following his downfall. Leftist elements he deemed responsible for the overthrow of the provisional government were attacked, and much of the *Conseiller* consequently consists of political diatribes. Louis Napoleon, on the other hand, fares well until the eve of the coup d'état. Perhaps by backing his recent rival he hoped for a political comeback. Copious excerpts from past political speeches marked what was to become a pattern in later works by Lamartine—a constant defense of his policies in 1848.

IV   Les Foyers du peuple

Les Foyers du peuple was published periodically from 1851 to 1853 by Lamartine as a one-man production. In its pages appeared largely miscellaneous items, poems from previous editions and old political speeches. A visit to Pompeii is recalled, and the priest's job in modern society is outlined with the usual stress on progressive Christianity as distinguished from medieval superstition. The career of Murat, Napoleon's trusted general who later aspired to rule all Italy, is also treated.

V   Le Tailleur de pierres de Saint-Point

Le Tailleur de pierres de Saint-Point was published in 1851 by Lecou.

The stonecutter, Claude des Huttes, relates to Lamartine his love for Denise whom he is obliged to leave in order to make the tour required of apprentices in the trade. Upon his return, he discovers Denise is a widow with two children. During his absence she marries out of pity Claude's blind brother Gratien. Denise and Claude now plan to wed but, when Claude prepares fireworks for the wedding celebration, they explode, killing Denise and her children. Resigning himself to God's will, Claude dies sometime afterward.

Lamartine knew the peasants of Burgundy, where the story is set, but failed to capture their spirit and appreciate their patois. Consequently, Claude's speech is not that of a true-to-life stonecutter but a dull, pedantic monologue. The artisan's philosophy is merely a restatement of Jocelyn's belief in a kind God who exists everywhere and hears the prayers of the lowly.

Except for occasional, lush descriptions the tale added nothing to Lamartine's reputation. Readers were already familiar with his preachments on sorrowful resignation. While there is sincere sympathy for the poor, Lamartine provides no realistic details on their conditions and personal reactions to misery. Certainly Claude would be an unusually humble and uncomplaining worker at any period in history.

VI Nouvelles Confidences

The *Nouvelles Confidences* was published in 1851 by Lévy and formed a sequel to the *Confidences*. Excerpts from an unfinished epic poem, *Les Visions*, constituted part of the work. They are discussed in another chapter.

The *Nouvelles Confidences* provides further details on Lamartine's youth and his five sisters. There are vignettes of his two uncles, one who wants him to be a scientist and the Abbé de Lamartine, a worldly priest. The chief episode involves Saluce, a friend of Lamartine, and Regina, an Italian princess. Saluce falls in love with Regina, already married to an older man. He helps her to escape to France where Lamartine shelters her. Imprisoned on charges brought by Regina's husband, Saluce agrees to give her up to save her the anguish of scandal and exile. An embittered Regina denounces Saluce and begins to take an interest in Lamartine.

The *Nouvelles Confidences* gives us more information about Lamartine's family background and hence is of some value. Otherwise, the work lacks the occasionally pleasing narrative style of the *Confidences*. The episode concerning Regina and Saluce is so much Romantic twaddle designed to make an Italian princess Lamartine met once in Italy alluring and mysterious. Especially silly is the ending, with Regina easily switching her affections to Lamartine after a passionate affair with Saluce.

Obviously, Lamartine was already trapped by the demands of publication for profit.

VII   Le Civilisateur

Le Civilisateur was published from 1852 to 1854 in Paris by Lamartine. Its express purpose was to educate the workingman through biographies of great men in history.

Homer and Milton are singled out as two great poets of all time. The Greek poet was so universal and profound that his works alone could easily give any reader a sound moral and cultural background. Milton, one of the illustrious poets of Christianity, excelled in poetizing the Bible and had a record blemished only by his defense of Cromwell.

Two outstanding heroes of Rome were Caesar and Cicero. The latter symbolized unflinching devotion to duty, opposed Catiline's conspiracy, and, despite differences, respected Caesar. Cicero's death for an honest decision to support Brutus amounted to martyrdom. While Caesar did not measure up to Cicero in Lamartine's estimation, he was more resourceful than Napoleon. Able and ambitious, he overcame a weak opponent, Pompey, only to meet the fate of so many dictators.

From the Middle Ages and early Renaissance Lamartine chooses a variety of figures—two lovers, a saint, and a patriot. In overthrowing Hapsburg rule William Tell became the Swiss George Washington. Joan of Arc's greatest miracle was her inner strength, not the miraculous power ascribed to her by superstition. On a human level, the story of Abelard and Héloïse was deeply moving in the warm, personal relationship of later years that followed a youthful passion.

Gutenberg represented to Lamartine a transition between medieval and modern times. Since the French poet felt language was of divine origin, it took Gutenberg's genius to perfect a process that would facilitate the recording of the spoken and written word.

A contemporary of Gutenberg, Christopher Columbus, excited Lamartine's imagination. The restless and melancholy Genoan had all the traits of a Romantic hero. Through his voyages of discovery he worked for the unity of mankind. The hardy explorer with his fanatical religious zeal somehow fitted into a divine plan not yet fully revealed by God to mankind.

Long before Columbus, Socrates experienced the frustrations of an endless quest to discover truth and died in the attempt. Lamartine's chapter on Socrates restates the central theme of *La Mort de Socrate*.

Philosophers, explorers, and generals do not monopolize the pages of *Le Civilisateur*, where space is devoted as well to two master craftsmen, Bernard Palissy and Joseph Jacquard. Palissy, who saw the hand of God everywhere, recorded this impression quite vividly in his pottery; as Palissy suffered for being a Huguenot, so did Jacquard become the victim of narrow-mindedness. Workers feared his mechanical loom would take away their jobs, but his ideals of art and industry persevered even though tragedy struck in the death of his wife and son.

Far removed from Europe, Antar, Arab warrior-poet of the sixth century, put down in his verses the feelings experienced in combat. Even in death Antar's body mounted on his faithful steed terrified enemies. His memory was honored by Arabs accustomed to venerating their poets.

A warrior better known to Europe was Cromwell, dubbed by Lamartine the Mohammed of the North. As a bloodthirsty dictator and loving father Cromwell presents an enigma to Lamartine, who sympathizes with Charles I. Like an Old Testament judge he could execute his daughter's lover without compunction and unite the British Empire through the strength of his personality and leadership. Lamartine thinks the French Revolution would have succeeded under Cromwell.

Another English leader, Nelson, also offered a study in paradox. His distinguished naval career contrasts embarrassingly with the affair with Lady Hamilton. Their love had a sanguinary effect on the treatment of Neapolitan rebels. Nelson's ruthless conduct here is blamed by Lamartine on the advice of Lady Hamilton.

More at home in discussing French letters, Lamartine picks Madame de Sévigné and Fénelon to illustrate the literary attainments of the seventeenth century. Madame de Sévigné's genius enabled her to become the Petrarch of French prose. Bossuet had the same power and pleasant imagery in his sermons. While Bossuet had a salutary influence on the French court, he was intolerant on the question of Fénelon and quietism. Of a more gentle disposition, Fénelon reminded Lamartine of the Greek philosophers. In *Télémaque* Fénelon took too utopian a view of human nature and tried too hard to imitate Homer. Still as a treatise on society and education *Télémaque* was superior to Rousseau's *Emile*.

Lamartine is at his best when writing on the literature of his own country and displays considerable sensitivity to the peculiar genius of French Classicism. When dealing with the thorny problem of the quietism controversy, he tends to be simplistic in assigning the major blame to Bossuet.

Less objective is his interpretation of historical figures outside France. Nelson's role in the Naples affair and Lady Hamilton's involvement are still moot questions. Cicero was a political opportunist who probably sealed his own fate, and Caesar was not simply a power-mad general. Milton pointed out the dangers of one-man rule to Cromwell, a level-headed leader inclined to be tolerant once peace was established. On the basis of available evidence, Gutenberg was not just an idealistic inventor but a fairly sharp businessman.

Lamartine's Romantic imagination is put to better use with subjects like Joan of Arc and Héloïse and Abelard. His interpretation of Joan of Arc is not essentially at variance with modern opinion, and the general outline of the romance of Héloïse and Abelard fits the known facts. His imagination is also given free rein in the treatment of Homer, where Lamartine airs his views on the preternatural powers of poetry. Almost no imagination at all is displayed in the pedestrian sketches of Antar, William Tell, Jacquard, Palissy, and Socrates.

The most interesting study is that of Columbus where Lamartine, in speaking of those men selected to carry out certain phases of God's plan, seems to identify himself with the explorer. Recent scholarship would appear to confirm Lamartine's interpretation of Columbus as a quasi-Romantic type convinced he was fulfilling a prophetic role. Other vignettes, while they may provide an occasionally provocative statement by Lamartine, are more often reiterative and written in a watered-down encyclopedic style.

VIII   Histoire de la Restauration

The *Histoire de la Restauration* was published in 1852 by Lecou.

Chateaubriand's role in the first days of the Restoration is outlined as well as the disruption caused by Napoleon's return. After Waterloo Lamartine pictures a weary Louis XVIII plagued by Orleanist ambitions, the rivalry of Fouché and Talleyrand, and the White Terror. The execution of Ney, the murder of the Duc de Berry, and the fall of Decazes' ministry coincided with the rise of anti-Bourbonist feeling. Napoleon's death revived Bonapartism. Louis XVIII made mistakes, concedes Lamartine, but paved the way for constitutional government. In recalling his own personal contact with Charles X and the Prince de Polignac, Lamartine attributes good intentions to them both. Failure to keep up with the times brought the collapse of Charles X.

Lamartine's work on the Restoration does not maintain the lively, narrative pace of the *History of the Girondists*. Apparently the period did not interest him as much as the Revolution of 1789 in which he saw an object lesson for France. The series of vignettes that enlivened the *History of the Girondists* finds no suitable counterpart here. Conversations reportedly taking place between Lamartine and leading figures in government are doubtless embellished to the benefit of the writer's own prestige. Although an eyewitness to events, Bourbonist sympathies kept him from seeing all the shortcomings of Louis XVIII and the obstinacy of Charles X. Since Lamartine was increasingly anti-Socialist after 1850, he may have felt the Bourbons were preferable to mob agitators.

IX   Nouveau Voyage en orient

The *Nouveau Voyage en orient* was published in 1853 by Lévy after Lamartine made a second journey to the Near East to inspect some property given to him by the Sultan of Turkey.

Lamartine recalls first his previous trip. The voyage to his destination is a record of personal impressions of the sea and a description of his ship companions. Constantinople with its exotic crowds and open marketplaces is considered in detail.

At the sultan's colorful court he visits the young ruler Abdul
Medjid. In visits elsewhere in Turkey, officials and peasants
are uniformly cordial and philosophical. The rest of the book is
a review of Turkish history in the first half of the nineteenth
century.

The *Nouveau Voyage en orient* is dull by comparison to the
original with its character portraits and philosophical observations. Lamartine unhappily still deems himself a man of importance as he relates his meetings with Turkish bigwigs. The
second half of the book with the pointless survey of recent
Turkish history is padding in the worst sense.

X   Histoire des Constituants

The *Histoire des Constituants* was published in four volumes
in 1855 by Lecou in Paris and treated the first part of the
Revolution up to the time the Girondists came to power.

The Constituent Assembly was the first of its kind convened
by a French king. Once in session it was only a matter of time
until all class distinctions were abolished and each delegate given
an equal voice. Public opinion, influenced by the affair of the
Diamond Necklace in 1785, was dead set against the queen.
The king meant well but was ineffectual. At this juncture, Mirabeau entered upon the scene and soon made his presence felt.
Necker was one of Mirabeau's chief rivals, and the latter sought
to undermine him. Mirabeau also had to contend with Lafayette,
who controlled the National Guard. To stay in power Mirabeau
had to rely on intrigue and compromise. The mob also posed a
problem by making the royal family move from Versailles to
the Tuileries and by invading the Chamber to force its will on
the Assembly.

In the Assembly Mirabeau faced the Abbé Maury, fiery spokesman of the Right, and the Abbé Sieyès, champion of the Left.
Financial problems unsolved by Necker and the demand to
expropriate Church property further complicated matters. A
flurry of pamphlets from underground presses and the mush-
rooming of political clubs added to the tension.

European nations in the meantime were forming a coalition
against the French Revolution. Mirabeau had always urged in

private the royal family to flee the country, although publicly he supported the policies of the National Assembly. The constant strain on his person caused Mirabeau to die suddenly in 1791. Lamartine closes with a tribute to Mirabeau's services to France and to the Constituent Assembly as well.

The *Histoire des Constituants* occasionally recaptures some of the sweep of the *Histoire des Girondins* with intimate sketches and stirring accounts of isolated incidents. The attack on the Bastille is noteworthy for the quality, color, and vivacity of the description. Like many a Romantic, Lamartine can envision the larger, physical proportions of an event but has difficulty arriving at psychological insights. The portrait of Mirabeau has validity as an impression of a public figure whose actions and decisions affected the Revolution, but an exhaustive study of Mirabeau's motives is beyond Lamartine. The author does succeed at least in outlining the role of Mirabeau and the opposition of Necker and Lafayette. In general, his estimate of them remains valid today. Mirabeau did play both ends against the middle in an effort to placate the mob and still remain in royal favor. Necker and Lafayette were equally concerned about their reputation.

The *Histoire des Constituants* acquires a certain unity from the emphasis placed on Mirabeau's role but at the expense of a well-rounded study of all the notables involved in the drama of 1789. As usual, needless quotations and digressions mar the overall effect. More time should have been devoted to clarifying individual motives and the events. But Lamartine seems more concerned with inviting comparison between Mirabeau's leadership and oratory and his own performance in 1848. Obsession with his downfall led to the almost incessant brooding on the subject in the works of his final period.

XI Histoire de la Russie

The *Histoire de la Russie* was published in 1855 by Perrotin. Lamartine was always concerned about the threat posed by the Russian bear, and it was only forty years since Napoleon's retreat from Moscow. The situation in the Crimea also added to the work's topicality.

Lamartine describes the times before Peter the Great as primitive and deistic and traces the nation's growth through the Tartar invasions, the turbulent reign of Ivan the Terrible, and the ruthless but enlightened rule of Peter the Great. Catherine had only grand ambitions and, Lamartine feels, does not measure up to Voltaire's praise of her. Through Kutuzov's defeat of Napoleon, Alexander I liberated Europe only to subject it to the tyranny of the Holy Alliance. Under Nicholas I little progress toward reform was seen.

Lamartine makes no significant or original judgments. The notion that despotism suits a country of Russia's size is patently taken from Montesquieu. Consisting largely of stale ideas and trivia the book is encumbered by long-winded quotations. Lamartine's dislike of Kutuzov smacks somewhat of chauvinism, and his attempt to emulate the incisive style of Voltaire's histories fails woefully. Along with the *Histoire de la Turquie* the work on Russia is a pitiful reminder of Lamartine's reduction to the miserable necessity of hack writing. Lack of sufficient documentation was a shortcoming for which Mérimée assailed Lamartine unmercifully.

XII   Histoire de la Turquie

The *Histoire de la Turquie* was published in 1855 by Hachette. Lamartine took an interest in that country on the basis of his visits there and his pro-Turkish posture when in the Chamber.

The work begins with Mohammed's rise as a leader of desert tribes. When the Turks embraced Islamism the history of Turkey formally began and was marked by continual wars. Following the Tartar threat under Tamurlane, Mohammed I and Mohammed II extended the empire to the Balkans and Mediterranean. Under Suleiman the Magnificent expansion continued into Central Europe. Selim II was defeated at Lepanto, and there began a gradual decline, hastened by Sobieski's victory at Vienna. Austria and Russia were persistent adversaries in the eighteenth century. With the nineteenth century, Turkey opposed Napoleon's invasion of Egypt. The country's misfortunes were characterized by the Greek revolt, the naval defeat at Navarino, and the janizaries' suppression in 1826. Mehemet Ali's challenge to Turkey typified the precarious position of a weakened nation formerly a great power in the Near East.

Lamartine has little understanding of the Turkish mind. Thoughout the work there is the unmistakable impression he is paraphrasing standard references on Turkey. What results is a lifeless summary of historical facts and little more. Lamartine is at his discursive worst and passes many superficial judgments. One quality counterbalancing these shortcomings is the author's endeavor to see the good points of the Turkish people and their beliefs.

XIII Cours familier de littérature

Lamartine began publication of the *Cours familier de littérature* in 1856. It was a miscellany on a variety of subjects that appeared in regular installments until 1869, the year of Lamartine's death. In all, twenty-eight volumes were published on literary criticism, history, biography, philosophy, theology, and topics of general interest. Each volume consisted of *entretiens,* a term Lamartine used to justify a chatty tone and frequent digressions.

Friends of Lamartine complimented him on the first volume. A committee of writers and critics backed his initial efforts. Friendly reviewers called him a second La Harpe, while hostile ones dismissed the whole venture as another attempt at hack writing to pay off the poet's debts. A publicity campaign launched in Europe and North and South America failed to win a large number of subscribers. The *Cours familier,* nevertheless, had a modest sale and assured Lamartine much-needed funds to satisfy impatient creditors.

A résumé of the contents of each volume is given below except for two poems, *Le Désert* and *La Vigne et la maison,* and two prose selections, *Le Père Dutemps* and *Fior d'Aliza,* summarized in subsequent discussions.

Volume I

Entretien I. Lamartine recalls the study of Cicero at Belley and the liberal Abbé Dumont, the model for Jocelyn.
Entretien II. The life of the literary and social figure Delphine

Gay (Madame Girardin) is related. The evolution of language
from primitive times is outlined as an uneven process of development.
Entretien III. Hinduism is pictured as one of the world's great
religions. Lamartine records his admiration of the Vedas and
friendship with the Baron d'Eckstein, a student of Hinduism.
Entretien IV. The development of poetry is traced, and the
preternatural operation of this divine gift is analyzed. Hebrew
and Hindu poetry exemplify primitive lyrics at their best.
Entretien V. The Unfortunate Brahmin and the Hindu drama,
Sacountala, are summarized and discussed.
Entretien VI. Hindu plays do not end in tragedy. Lovers are
usually absorbed into the divine essence.

Volume II

Entretien VII. Literature with its alternate periods of glory and
decline disproves the theory of progress. Readers are reminded
how Lamartine in 1848 prevented war in Italy.
Entretien VIII. No great epic has yet appeared in modern times.
In a discussion of French Classicism the author praises Bossuet
and criticizes La Fontaine's cynicism.
Entretien IX. The Second Republic did not heed the lessons of
1789 and thus failed. Thanks to the genius of Voltaire, Rousseau,
and Buffon the eighteenth century was a brilliant period.
Entretien X. Lamartine recalls meeting Byron and Gibbon and
his contacts with Chateaubriand, Balzac, Vigny, and Sainte-
Beuve.
Entretien XI. The text of "Le Désert" is given and compared to
"Le Désespoir." Lamartine tells how the Book of Job inspired
both poems.
Entretien XII. Job personifies the mystery of man's destiny. The
dominant faculty in man is conscience, an innate function that
regulates intelligence and sentiment, the other two operations
of the mind.

Volume III

Entretien XIII. The highlights of Racine's career are considered—
the success of *Athalie* and *Esther* and the narrow framework
of Classical tragedy.

Entretien XIV. Lamartine rates Racine's sublimity over Shakespeare's grandeur and reminisces about Talma, the great interpreter of Racinian roles.
Entretien XV. "La Vigne et la maison" and "Le Père Dutemps" appear in this section.
Entretien XVI. Lamartine deplores the average Frenchman's cultural chauvinism. Even the keen critical spirit of Boileau has this shortcoming.
Entretien XVII. Frédéric Ozanam, a good Dante scholar, understood the timeless philosophy of the Italian poet.
Entretien XVIII. Musset, lacking the religious sensibility of his contemporaries, failed to realize his full potential.

Volume IV

Entretien XIX. The charm of the *Nuits* is a welcome relief from Musset's usual cynicism.
Entretien XX. Lamartine summarizes Dante's *Divine Comedy* and comments on its sublimity marred here and there by melodramatic episodes.
Entretien XXI. To Lamartine Béranger had a talent more Grecian in spirit than Gallic.
Entretien XXII. Béranger reflects the spirit of his times.
Entretiens XXIII and XXIV. Lamartine tells how he developed an interest in poetry at Belley, compares poetry to music and painting, and describes how his mother taught him about Homer.

Volume V

Entretiens XXV and XXVI. The main action of the Iliad is summarized as well as the life of Homer.
Entretien XXVII. Poetry is a divine function and indefinable. It sets the poet apart from other men.
Entretien XXVIII. Pindar was the first of the great secular poets, while David was one of the most sublime sacred poets.
Entretien XXIX. The compositions of Mozart reveal a power of expression superior to the written word. Rossini also has this gift.
Entretien XXX. Despite the limits of instruments and voices

as descriptive media, Mozart imparted a graphic quality to his operas.

Volume VI

Entretiens XXXI and XXXII. Petrarch was a Romantic beset by melancholy who sang the divine praises.
Entretien XXXIII. David is judged superior to Pindar.
Entretiens XXXIV and XXXV. Unlike Socrates, Confucius proposes a just, reasonable government.
Entretien XXXVI. Lamartine treats the aims and techniques of painting and examines Léopold Robert's work.

Volume VII

Entretien XXXVII. Robert's use of visual effects shows the relationship of painting to poetry.
Entretiens XXXVIII and XXXIX. Lamartine admits the influence of Goethe's *Werther* on him and that *Faust* affected the portrayal of Jocelyn.
Entretien XL. Adolphe Dumas, author of *La Cueillette des Olives,* has the Provençal genius of Mistral.
Entretien XLI. The theory of *l'art pour l'art,* too narrow in scope, would not satisfy Goethe who with Schiller personifies the individualistic and mystical spirit of Germany.
Entretien XLII. Joseph de Maistre, despite the fanaticism of his views, excites Lamartine's admiration.

Volume VIII

Entretien XLIII. The *Soirées de Saint-Pétersbourg* by de Maistre is discussed and analyzed.
Entretiens XLIV to XLVI. Lamartine pays tribute to Thiers' *History of the Empire* but regrets the undue praise of Napoleon.
Entretiens XLVII and XLVIII. Finding both Horace and La Fontaine licentious, Lamartine judges the former a superior artist.

Volume IX

Entretiens XLIX to LI. The salon of Madame Récamier brings back memories of her friendship with Chateaubriand and of the celebrities she entertained.

Entretiens LII and LIII. The *Prince* of Machiavelli is a commentary on the court of César Borgia. Since Machiavelli's time, Italy has experienced the agony of internal dissension, foreign intervention, and the papal question.

Entretien LIV. As a solution to Italian problems Lamartine proposes a United States of Italy.

Volume X

Entretiens LV and LVI. The author recalls his first reading of Ariosto and then summarizes and analyzes *Orlando Furioso.*

Entretien LVII. The young poet, Victor La Prade, shared Lamartine's interest in Rossini and in the *Imitation of Christ.*

Entretien LVIII. The problems of the early 1850's and the advice and help of friends then are remembered by Lamartine.

Entretiens LIX and LX. Talleyrand worked for peace just as Lamartine did in 1848.

Volume XI

Entretien LXI. To counter the expansion of Russia and Prussia, Lamartine proposes a Franco-Austrian alliance.

Entretiens LXII to LXIV. Cicero dominated his period by the eloquence displayed in the anti-Catilinian orations. He was a moralist and spokesman for liberty.

Entretiens LXV to LXVI. Rousseau, though a superb stylist, is guilty of dangerous and childish notions in *Emile* and the *Contrat Social.* The principle of the general will undermines society and individual rights.

Volume XII

Conclusion of Entretien LXVI; Entretien LXVII. Rousseau overlooks man's moral nature and the divine origin of society. Under the influence of Confucius, China encouraged the growth of morality.

Entretiens LXVIII and LXIX. Tacitus gives a vivid picture of Roman society with moral judgments and insights.

Entretiens LXX to LXXII. The *Histoire des Girondins,* Lamartine feels, helped to overthrow Louis-Philippe. In warning France about the mistakes of 1789 Lamartine pointed the way to peaceful revolution.

Volume XIII

Entretiens LXXIII to LXXV. Lamartine tells how in 1848 he tried to avoid the Girondists' errors. He admits being too hard on Danton. Marat, Danton, and Charlotte Corday exemplified the brilliant personalities of the Revolution.
Entretiens LXXVI and LXXVII. Lamartine reminisces about his friendship with Louis de Ronchaud and praises the latter's *Phidias* and views on the clarity and order of Graeco-Roman art as opposed to the Gothic.
Entretien LXXVIII. Count Marcellus' diplomatic career is presented, with a digression on Lamartine's visit to Lady Stanhope.

Volume XIV

Entretien LXXIX. Lamartine considers Count Marcellus' opinion of Chateaubriand and his own as well.
Entretien LXXX. Lamartine treats the poetry of Adolphe Dumas.
Entretiens LXXXI and LXXXII. Like the Bible, Plato's thought, according to Lamartine, comes from a more primitive revelation. The political theory of Plato seems dangerously utopian to Lamartine.
Entretiens LXXXIII and LXXXIV. Lamartine writes about his friendship with Hugo. *Les Misérables* has a murderer for its hero and a deist posing as a bishop.

Volume XV

Entretiens LXXXV to LXXXVII. The Battle of Waterloo, depicted in stirring fashion, and the flight through the sewers typify the good and bad points of *Les Misérables.* Lamartine finds Hugo too one-sided in favoring the proletariat.
Entretiens LXXXVIII to XC. Eugénie de Guérin's deeply religious upbringing is seen in her letters and poems.

Volume XVI

Entretiens XCI to XCIII. Tasso's early life and imprisonment are described. Lamartine considers Tasso's style vivid and his characters a reflection of the writer's own sufferings.
Entretiens XCIV and XCV. Lamartine lauds the stoicism of Vigny's "Moïse," the charming pathos of *Chatterton,* and the sense of duty in *Servitude et grandeur militaires.*
Entretien XCVI. Details of the life of Vittorio Alfieri are given.

Volume XVII

Entretiens XCVII and XCVIII. Pretentiousness spoiled Alfieri's style. His *Saül* inspired Lamartine's play by the same name.
Entretiens XCIX and C. Cellini was a great artist characterized by the naïveté of his emotions and deeds.
Entretiens CI and CII. Lamartine comments favorably on Sainte-Beuve's poetry, digresses to relate a discussion he had personally with Stendhal, and then admits he failed in *Raphaël* to reconcile earthly and divine love. Sainte-Beuve met a similar failure in *Volupté.* Contrary to Sainte-Beuve, Lamartine does not think that true epic poetry is the product of a primitive era.

Volume XVIII

Entretiens CIII to CV. Aristotle is more realistic than Rousseau in sizing up the people's volatility. His *Poetics* have endured despite shortcomings. Newton proved the validity of Aristotle's *Physics.*
Entretiens CVI to CVIII. In Balzac Lamartine discerns a religious temperament. *Eugénie Grandet* compares favorably with psychological studies in Molière, Plautus, and Terence. *Père Goriot* starts out well but has the ending of a second-rate novel.

Volume XIX

Entretiens CIX to CXI. Cardinal Consalvi's life points up the conflict of temporal and spiritual interests in Rome. He served Pius VII faithfully in dealing with Napoleon.
Entretiens CXII to CXV. The scientist Alexander Humboldt produced notable results in the field of mineralogy. In his theory of the physical world, however, he omits God.

Volume XX

Entretien CXVI. Lamartine compares Xavier de Maistre's *Le Lépreux de la Cité d'Aoste* to Job and Rousseau.
Entretien CXVII. Audubon is French, not American. Lamartine defends the invasion of Mexico as a step against Yankee imperialism already attempting to subdue the Confederate states.
Entretien CXVIII. Long quotations from Audubon are used to illustrate his contributions.
Entretiens CXIX and CXX. Johann Eckermann's *Conversations with Goethe* is quoted at length.

Volume XXI

Entretien CXXI. Voltaire lacked the spiritual insights of Goethe, who became more religious in his last years.
Entretien CXXII. Lamartine admires the *Imitation of Christ*.
Entretien CXXIII. In introducing *Fior d'Aliza* Lamartine looks back on his literary activity in the 1820's, his marriage, and his trip to Italy.
Entretiens CXXIV to CXXVI. Text of *Fior d'Aliza*.

Volume XXII

Entretiens CXXVII to CXXX. Continuation of *Fior d'Aliza*.
Entretiens CXXXI to CXXXII. Excerpts are quoted from Turgenev's *Two Friends* and *Two Days in the Forest*.

Volume XXIII

Entretien CXXXIII. In Turgenev Lamartine senses the power of a writer from a country whose literature has yet to develop.
Entretien CXXXIV. Lamartine quotes from and comments on the poems of Clotilde de Surville.
Entretiens CXXXV and CXXXVI. The warm human quality of Erckmann and Chatrian is revealed in *Friend Fritz* and the *History of a Conscript of 1813*.
Entretien CXXXVII. Lamartine reminisces about Milly and Saint-Point.
Entretien CXXXVIII. Lamartine expostulates on the pristine vigor of the *Nibelungenlied* with excerpts.

Volume XXIV

Entretien CXXXIX. Further quotations from the *Nibelungenlied* are given.

Entretiens CXL and CXLI. Bernardin de Saint-Pierre's *Paul et Virginie* proved popular with the general public. Aimé Martin pays a fitting tribute to Saint-Pierre.

Entretiens CXLII and CXLIII. Jean Chardin in the seventeenth century wrote the type of travel literature Lamartine liked.

Entretien CXLIV. During the 1820's Lamennais' *Essay on Indifference* had a strong effect on Lamartine.

Volume XXV

Entretiens CXLV and CXLVI. Macpherson was too conscientious to alter drastically the works of Ossian.

Entretiens CXLVII to CXLIX. Lamartine takes a look at the stormy period of the Medicis and Savonarola.

Entretien CL. Le Misanthrope is an excellent play with an artificial ending. *Tartuffe* is Molière's masterpiece.

Volume XXVI

Entretien CLI. Molière and Shakespeare are compared in light of their respective periods.

Entretien CLII to CLIV. Corinne reflects Madame de Staël's struggle with Napoleon. *De l'Allemagne* was a manifesto against materialism and tyranny. The *Considérations sur la révolution française* only envisioned government by property owners.

Entretien CLV. In his paintings Michelangelo presents his own version of the *Divine Comedy.*

Entretien CLVI. Mary Stuart's association with Bothwell and conflict with Knox come under Lamartine's scrutiny.

Volume XXVII

Entretien CLVII. Lamartine concludes the story of Mary Stuart.

Entretien CLVIII. Lamartine takes issue with Montesquieu's theory of climate and interpretation of Oriental customs.

Entretien CLIX. Herodotus was not the first historian. Homer and Moses preceded him.

Entretien CLX. Lamartine writes about old friends, the Marquise de Raigecourt and the Duc de Rohan.
Entretiens CLXI and CLXII. Lamartine feels critics underrate the beauty of *Atala. René* is reviewed and its influence discussed. The effect of the *Génie du Christianisme* on its times is also related.

Volume XXVIII

Entretiens CLXIII to CLXV. Chateaubriand's conversion, while sincere, stemmed from emotional factors. He failed to produce an epic poem in *Les Martyrs* but brought musicality to the French language.
Entretien CLXVI. Voltaire fought intolerance but denied the existence of a personal God. *Mahomet,* his best play, gives an inaccurate picture of Mohammed.
Entretien CLXVII. Through the divine language of poetry the poet interprets the works of God. Poetry divinizes man and expresses his relationship with the Creator.
Entretien CLXVIII. Télémaque is interpreted as Christian in inspiration and pagan in form. Fénelon's relations with Madame Guyon and the dispute over quietism are detailed.

XIV   *Analysis*

The *Cours familier de littérature* has no claim to greatness simply because it consists of twenty-eight volumes. Much of the material evidently was borrowed from ready sources such as encyclopedias, popular histories, and dictionaries. The volumes represent nevertheless the chief literary work of Lamartine in the last fourteen years of his life. Toward the end, his niece, Valentine, and secretary, Charles Alexandre, probably got out the final editions, assembling whatever available material there was in the poet's files. This would account for an occasional inconsistency in viewpoint; for example, the final volume has two different opinions on Voltaire, one favorable, the other not.

Unquestionably the most significant pages contain the poems, "Le Désert" and "La Vigne et la maison," and Lamartine's definition of poetry and its function. "La Vigne et la maison" proves that his poetic powers had not failed, and "Le Désert" provides valuable insights into the last phase of his religious thinking. From Lamartine's concept of the poet's privileged position readers acquire some understanding of the lofty manner and tone too often dismissed as sheer arrogance. He felt in all sincerity he was performing a ritual in honor of the deity.

Details provided by Lamartine on India and China seem outdated today. His remarks on India are important in relation to the Baron d'Eckstein, who first acquainted him with Hinduism. In the *Cours familier* Lamartine showed a continued interest in Vedic literature, to which he was initially introduced by Eckstein and Guigniaut's translation of Creuzer. From an analysis of Indic letters the poet sought to establish one of his favorite ideas, the pristine quality of some of the earliest writing known to mankind.

On the writers of French Classicism Lamartine has the Classicist's admiration of clear and concise style. His preference for Graeco-Roman art and architecture over the Gothic also attests to strong Classical leanings. Still, on the subject of contemporaries—Hugo, Vigny, and Musset—he defends the spontaneous character of inspiration.

Further understanding of Lamartine's literary views may be obtained from his remarks on the novel. He liked Balzac's portrayal of human emotions in which the novelist displayed a talent worthy of Plautus, Terence, and Molière. *Les Misérables* with its stress on poverty and misery displeased him. Anything smacking of Realism or Naturalism had little appeal to Lamartine who relished, however, Hugo's colorful word picture of Waterloo.

Comparative literature was definitely not Lamartine's strong point. Russian and American writers seemed to him to be laboring under primitive conditions, and there is no mention of Spain. His impressions of Italian writers appear derived in large part from secondary sources. While appreciative of Goethe, he makes no original judgments; only his personal reaction to Goethe is of any value. In fact, his lukewarm treatment of Boileau and Sainte-Beuve discloses an indifference to formal literary criticism. There is some merit to his comparison of Molière and Shakespeare, one of the few times he formulates a serious judgment and is not content to record merely personal impressions.

One aspect of the *Cours familier*, generally overlooked, is the poet's liking for Mozart. Lamartine was attracted to a composer with the ability to transmit through sound graphic impressions of an intellectually stimulating nature. Lamartine, perhaps unconsciously, tried to impart to his poetry some of the quality of Mozart's music.

When dealing with contemporaries in the Romantic movement Lamartine was reasonably objective. He had strong likes and dislikes, but a basic generosity enabled him to see merit in literary views and methods opposed to his. Disapproval of *Les Misérables* did not make him lose sight of Hugo's genius. Lamartine valued highly Musset's talent despite the latter's irreligious flippancy, and he respected the sublimity of Vigny's lyrics. Chateaubriand, with whom he did not enjoy a warm relationship, received due recognition for his role in French Romanticism. Lamartine esteemed the versatility of Madame de Staël and even the creative powers of the dogmatic Joseph de Maistre. The contemporary writers approved by Lamartine had on the whole Classical or Romantic traits. His aversion to the school of art for art's sake made him avoid any mention of the Parnassians.

Personal reflections by Lamartine are an important feature of the *Cours familier*. Many sections are welcome additions to documents on the literary and social figures of Romanticism. Accounts of boyhood friendships and memories of Belley aid the researcher. In spite of the subjective slant of many of Lamartine's observations, these recollections throw light on attitudes and contacts at given periods in the poet's life.

Defense of his policy in 1848 leads to unexpected digressions. His proposed solution to the Italian problem was unfeasible, and his support of Napoleon III's Mexican venture and the Confederacy an astonishing volte-face. More perceptive are his predictions on future threats to peace in Europe and of the dangers of Prussian militarism and Russian expansionism. The concept of Austria as a buffer to Prussia and Russia was suggested after World War I.

In the area of philosophy Lamartine's conclusions are predictable. He prefers the Platonic concept of the real existence of ideas to Aristotelian ideogenesis with its stress on the senses. In political philosophy he opts for Aristotle's well-ordered state and opposes, with bitter remembrances of 1848, Plato's fanciful notion of a republic. The ruling faculty in man, Lamartine maintains, is conscience, an intuitive function that preempts rationalization and leads directly to moral truth. Although this latter concept appeared reasonable to Lamartine in the abstract, he was cautious about applying it on a broad basis. Disillusionment with the masses made him wary of utopian schools relying on the instinct of all men to do good.

Even in the religious sphere pessimism affected Lamartine's outlook. "Le Désert" clearly illustrates the extent of that pessimism in the conclusion that man has limited knowledge of the workings of a mysterious God. "La Vigne et la maison" speaks by contrast of a clement Providence but with an air of sadness and resignation. This life is a vale of tears compensated for only by eternal life. In regard to Catholicism, Lamartine treats the Church kindly in the discussion of Consalvi and the papacy. He applauds Voltaire's stand against intolerance but spurns the redoubtable cynic's lack of faith.

The *Cour familier de littérature* furnishes much of interest to students of Lamartine and is a valuable document of the last phase of his career. The twenty-eight volumes, interspersed with long quotations, are of uneven quality and often repetitious. Caution, therefore, must be exercised in examining their contents.

XV *"Le Désert, ou L'Immaterialité de Dieu"*

"Le Désert, ou L'Immaterialité de Dieu," was published in 1856 in the second volume of the *Cours familier.*

In the desert at night the poet meditates on Job's trials and asks God to appear to him as He did formerly to Job. A voice within the poet denounces such a request; it is God refusing to surrender His immateriality. Why should He willingly destroy His omnipotence? Since the efforts of all organized religions to explain His essence have failed, God tells Lamartine that Mystery is the only adequate term by which to address Him. After this remonstrance, a trembling Lamartine ponders its meaning.

The deity speaking to Lamartine appears modern when denouncing superstition and yet reverts to Old Testament form when attacking pagan practices of ancient times:

And by what word do you want me to name myself for you? And
through what sense do you wish me to appear to man? The eye,
the ear, the mouth, or the hand? What is there of God in you?
What is there human about me?[1]

The revelation man once had at the beginning was soon
distorted: "Since the day on which Eden's light was extinguished,
mendacious antiquity depicted me in a dream."[2]
Metaphysical systems were all equally inadequate in their
definitions of God. Pantheism especially gave a chaotic view of
creation

Where God Himself is swallowed up in infinity, a brutal mixture of
confused elements in which good is no longer good and evil is
no longer evil. . . .[3]

At the end Lamartine submits without question to the Creator's
will: "O Mystery! I said to Him, well, thus be my faith. Mystery,
O sacred relation of the Creator to me!"[4]
If the poet's God insists on His immateriality, this insistence
does not rule out an intimate relationship with the Creator. There
is still a personal deity to whom Lamartine can pray. The creed
of "Le Désert" is simply Lamartine's progressive Christianity
minus the poet's earlier optimism. He still accepts the progressive
nature of revelation in God's truth illumining the reason but
sees it now more in terms of man's personal experience. The bitter lessons of 1848 make it impossible for Lamartine to envision
now the progress of the masses inspired by the moral precepts of
Christianity.
Lines interpreted by some critics as Voltairean in reality
reflect the general tone of the Book of Job. In the preface to "Le
Désert" Lamartine goes to great lengths to stress the importance
of Job's inspiration in its composition. Whatever Lamartine may
have thought about Catholicism at the time, there is nothing
to indicate that the emphasis on God's incorporeality is a direct
attack on the Eucharist. Lamartine is more interested in
emphasizing his own role as a modern Job.
From the standpoint of rhetoric, a comparison with Voltaire
is justifiable. In its heavy use of abstract and didactic terms "Le
Désert" recalls Voltaire's poems on philosophical matters. "Le

Désert" is a lucid expression of the poet's feelings and a creditable specimen of Romantic poetry on a philosophical theme. Its counterpart, "La Vigne et la maison," affords an interesting contrast with its return to a childlike faith. The two poems, like "Le Désespoir" and "La Foi," must be studied together for a complete picture of Lamartine's religious outlook in the final phase of his writings.

XVI *"La Vigne et la maison"*

"La Vigne et la maison" was published in 1857 in the third volume of the *Cours familier.*

Lamartine asks his soul the reason for its weariness. The soul replies that it longs for happier days. Recollections follow of blissful days at the family homestead. In the course of his reminiscing, Lamartine restates familiar themes from the *Méditations* and *Harmonies* as he perceives aspects of nature reflective of his own sorrow and regrets. The poet ends with the conviction that the spirit through faith finds repose in a beneficent Providence.

Free of the affectation formerly annoying even to admirers, Lamartine finds his spirit is in the mood only for a lamentation, not a hymn of joy:

I only like the hour of darkness on long days. I listen only to these funereal stanzas of the chants sobbed by the priest while leading a funeral procession.[5]

Lamartine uses again the successful techniques of the *Méditations.* Physical surroundings directly reflect his own feelings. The prayers for the dead led by the priest are part of a Chateaubriandesque formula that has a sincere note in the context of an old man's memories of youth and thoughts on approaching death. Eventide has always held charms for the poet: "This hour has soft impressions for our senses like muffled footsteps which tread upon moss."[6]

Sadness was a chronic condition in Lamartine. Reference in Catholic liturgy to life as a vale of tears was an axiom he took seriously. Accordingly, he preferred hours of the day and physical settings most in keeping with a mood of melancholy. There was also a preference on his part for pastel hues and serene land-scapes affected by soft rays of light, not sharp disagreeable effects. He had the sensitivity of a Romantic colored by the Classicist's need for order and tranquility. This very quality marks "Le Lac" and "La Vigne et la maison."

Unknowingly, when he inquires about the function of memory, Lamartine approaches those Romantic poets like Nodier and Nerval who concerned themselves with dreams and the sub-conscious:

You who made the memory, did you do so in order that people may forget? No, it is to give back to time at the end all its days, to have flow together beyond in a single current the past, the future, these two halves of life one of which says "Never" and the other "Always." This past, sweet Eden from which our soul came forth, is it not part of our eternity?[7]

Normally such questions as memory and the components of time were too sophisticated for Lamartine. In "La Vigne et la maison" he conceives of the past somehow as forming part of his essence; the sum total of experiences, past, present, and future gives him a fuller picture of man's life. As to be expected, Lamartine does not relegate such considerations to the limits of human speculation, but elevates them to the level of divinity where in the eternal order of things time has no meaning.

Having revisited scenes of childhood and praised the sanctity of the family, Lamartine addresses the God of Christianity and Rousseau, a deity apprehended by the heart, not comprehended by the mind. Larger social questions are no longer at issue. Only the immediate relationship of the poet and his loved ones to God matters. Now at the age of sixty-six Lamartine sees death in the offing and puts his faith in a benevolent Providence:

O gentle Providence! O mother of the family from whose home so many children swarm, and who, smiling in the midst, see them crying, remember, heart of heaven, that the earth is your daughter and man is a son of God![8]

With "La Vigne et la maison" Lamartine enters the final phase of his religious thinking. In "Le Désert" he realized the inability of metaphysical systems to arrive at an adequate definition of the deity and felt all human efforts to do so appeared futile. Only an acceptance in faith of God's omnipotence could be of spiritual benefit to the individual. "Le Désert" ends on a rather forlorn note, but "La Vigne et la maison" closes on one of hope. Once again Lamartine finds the warm, personal God of the *Méditations.* Social reform is forgotten as the regeneration of the individual alone concerns the poet.

From the standpoint of style, "La Vigne et la maison" is usually considered Lamartine's best poem. He uses to good effect a delicate musicality, outlines a landscape without harsh contrasts, and recaptures the joys of an uncomplicated childhood. His prayer to God is earnest and unaffected. It was fitting that after a long period of poetic inactivity Lamartine produced a poem that transcended everyday literary conventions to express basic human emotions in a simple straightforward way.

XVII   *"Le Père Dutemps"*

"Le Père Dutemps" was a short story originally written in 1848 and which appeared in the third volume of the *Cours familier* in 1857. Told in the form of a letter to a friend by Lamartine in November, 1848, it relates how the poet, weary of politics, withdraws to Saint-Point to reflect and rest. Revisiting the scenes of boyhood he meets an old egg-dealer, Père Dutemps. Now blind, the octogenarian symbolizes to Lamartine the spirit of sorrowful resignation. They part company after commiserating with one another. At the end of the narration Lamartine sees life from now on only as a vale of tears.

"Le Père Dutemps" strikes the lugubrious note seen in other overly sentimental writings of Lamartine. Of significance is the sincere feeling of nostalgia that penetrates the artificial melancholy and foreshadows the appealing lines of "La Vigne et la maison."

XVIII   La France Parlementaire

La France Parlementaire was published in six volumes in Paris by Lacroix in 1864-65.

The work covers highlights in Lamartine's political career in the Chamber in the form of addresses from the floor on a wide

variety of topics ranging from the sale of wine to foreign relations.
Just back from the Near East in 1834 he advocated support of
Turkey against Russia. Colonization and expansionism in Algeria,
he cautioned, should proceed at a moderate rate. As for relations
with America, Lamartine recommended payment for French
seizure of American ships in 1812. On the domestic front he
attacked anticlericalism and those opposed to social reform and
abolition of the death penalty. During the rest of the 1830's
he expanded the scope of his legislative concerns. The elimina-
tion of slavery, the dangers of censorship, and unilateral action
in foreign affairs were the objects of considerable discussion by
Lamartine. In the field of education he supported preservice
training of women teachers and the study of Classical languages.
As the decade ended, the return of Napoleon's remains ominously
foreshadowed a Bonapartist resurgence, and war still threatened
Europe. Lamartine sensed trouble at home and warned his colleagues that France was becoming restless.

In the period leading up to events in 1848 Lamartine continued to speak on every conceivable subject from the right of
writers to a living wage to a CIA-type operation by France in
Argentina. On the military potential of railroads he evoked
laughter by ridiculing one general's suggestion that in a battle
situation opposing troops could fire at each other from moving
trains. Speaking in a more serious vein, he advised against war-
like moves abroad. Among problems still with us today Lamartine
had to contend with fiscal sanity and undue restrictions on the
issuing of passports. He opposed the annexation of Texas by
the United States since it spelled the extension of slavery.

While serving in the Chamber Lamartine reminded constit-
uents back home of his devotion to their interests and his refusal
to become involved by allegiance to a particular political party.
With his advent to power in 1848 there was a flurry of speeches
to all segments of the population: students, sewer-workers, Freemasons, minority groups, foreign delegations. Foreign powers
were told France would not spread revolution beyond its borders.
When his prestige began to wane, Lamartine still defended his
policies aimed at maintaining order.

With the presidential election in the offing, Lamartine outlined the qualifications of the ideal candidate—a man dedicated

to representation of all the people. He told citizens of his home town at Mâcon that rural France was the nation's backbone unlike the volatile Parisian proletariat. His own decision to run for president was explained by Lamartine as a desire to give voters the widest possible choice. Defeated by Louis-Napoleon and now subjected to ridicule on the floor of the Chamber, he supported the new president and discounted talk of a coup d'état. After March 15, 1851, Lamartine retired from the Chamber but continued to comment on political developments. Denying any desire to run again for president, he found Louis-Napoleon preferable to a Bourbonist or Orieanist. A month before the coup d'état of December 2, 1851, he described how a ruthless leader could seize power. When Louis-Napoleon did that very thing, Lamartine announced his retirement from public life.

Much of *La France parlementaire* consists of gratuitous outpourings. From a stylistic standpoint there are occasional passages with a refinement in tone and coloring. Too often Lamartine's speeches are impaired by needless repetition and awkward handling of terminology in fields unfamiliar to the poet. The insertion in parentheses of cries of approbation recalls Tocqueville's remark that Lamartine indicated frequently wild applause when actually there was none. Tocqueville's charge becomes credible upon reading the long harangues and tedious recitations of facts.

If not the most accomplished politician, Lamartine managed nonetheless to stay in office about eighteen years. He was probably defeated more than once in debate but had inserted in the record remarks that pleased electors back home. In Mâcon when making firsthand reports to the voters Lamartine always stressed that, being a peasant at heart, he found it difficult to cope with city slickers.

The greatest defect in Lamartine's political strategy was the naïve overanxiousness he betrayed when the presidential contest drew near. By constantly justifying his policies as head of the provisional government, he probably contributed to his own defeat by Louis-Napoleon. Lamartine is most pathetic when, discredited with French voters, he slyly suggests himself nevertheless as an alternative to Bonaparte in the 1852 presidential elections.

Much of what Lamartine stood for had positive value. He abolished slavery and kept France out of war in 1848. Aware of the Prussian threat, he thought the rebuilding of Paris fortifications was useless in modern warfare. His objections to French interference in Spain were ultimately vindicated by the conflict of interests that led to war with Prussia. In the field of social reform Lamartine showed his best side. Fearful of radical overnight solutions, he supported sober legislation to aid the starving masses, orphans, and other forgotten members of society. He wanted to do away with capital punishment and reform the penal system. Among the later works of Lamartine, *La France parlementaire* supplies data on less familiar aspects of his thinking on political and social matters.

XIX   Civilisateurs et conquérants

Published in two volumes by Lacroix in Paris in 1865, *Civilisateurs et conquérants* is merely a selection of biographical sketches of figures most of whom are treated elsewhere in the *Cours familier* and similar works. The subjects considered range from Solon and Pericles to Peter the Great and Michelangelo. Readers already weary of such trite vignettes paid little heed to *Civilisateurs et conquérants*.

XX   Shakespeare et son œuvre

Shakespeare et son œuvre was published in Paris in 1864 by A. Lacroix and Verboeckhoven.

In a treatise consisting mainly of excerpts from well-known plays by Shakespeare, Lamartine gives a few brief impressions of the English playwright. Although lacking the comical genius of Molière and the elegance of Racine, Shakespeare, according to Lamartine, surpassed them both by the range of his creativity and profound grasp of human nature. Individual plays revealed to Lamartine good and bad points. The advice of the nurse to Juliet tainted the tender love story with what the French poet judged a note of obscenity. Hamlet's character fascinated Lamartine as well as the powerful though brutal study of Lady Macbeth's power over her husband. By comparison, *Othello* was just another melodrama with needless butchery in the final scene. The best example of Shakespeare's creation of a world of fantasy was *The Tempest.*

Shakespeare et son œuvre is of no broad significance except as evidence of Lamartine's reaction to the great playwright. The opinions expressed by Lamartine reveal his dramaturgic tastes to be primarily molded by French Classicism. Capable of sensing the sublimity of Shakespeare's power, Lamartine is, nonetheless, shocked by scenes he finds devoid of versimilitude with no observance of the proprieties as defined by the literary canons of seventeenth-century France.

XXI   *"William Pitt"* and *"Lord Chatham"*

"William Pitt" and "Lord Chatham" constituted part of a series of sketches, *Portraits et Biographies,* published in 1865 in Paris by A. Lacroix. The other vignettes were extracted from previous histories and biographies.

Chatham was the first of a long line of British orators and appeared at a time when England needed a powerful spokesman. Chatham guided his nation through the Seven Years' War but on two occasions displayed a lack of foresight by opposing American independence and the king's desire to unite England with Hanover and other German states. If the latter event had taken place then, reasons Lamartine, France would have had a strong ally against Russia in the nineteenth century.

William Pitt succeeded his father, Lord Chatham, and immediately met with strong opposition. He clashed with Lord North, Fox, Sheridan, and Burke. To placate the irascible George III, whose support he so desperately required, Pitt was obliged to abandon plans for religious freedom in Ireland and the abolition of slavery in British colonies. Lamartine credits Pitt with a correct analysis of the violence of the French Revolution and the threat posed by Napoleon.

For understandable reasons Lamartine identifies himself with the two brilliant orators, but his arguments on the power of the spoken word alone in politics are unconvincing. Hopelessly out of his field when dealing with English politics, Lamartine fails to comprehend the complicated situations faced by the two British statesmen. What Lamartine considers their crowning glory—the attempt to dominate the scene by their personalities and oratory— is considered by many historians their weak point. Both were solitary figures with few friends. Lamartine's study of Pitt and Chatham tells us more about his own convictions on the role of the silver-tongued speaker in government.

XXII   Fior d'Aliza

Fior d'Aliza was published in volumes XXI and XXII of the *Cours familer* in 1866 and included *Entretiens* 124 to 130.

Lamartine visits a peasant family near Lucca in Tuscany. A beautiful girl, Fior d'Aliza, lives with her child at the home of her father, Antonio. Her mother having died early, she was reared by her aunt with her cousin, Hyeronimo. Lamartine listens to the story of their sufferings at the hands of the brutal captain of the constabulary who lusts after Fior. When one of the constables wounds Fior, he is shot by Hyeronimo. Disguised as a boy, Fior sets out to find where her cousin is imprisoned and locates him after a series of adventures. They are married in prison, and Fior takes her husband's place to allow him to escape. When she is being led to execution Hyeronimo returns to save her. He is sent to the galleys and is eventually reunited with Fior d'Aliza and their child.

Fior d'Aliza represents no substantial change in Lamartine's limited attempts at novel-writing. The central figure, a comely Italian lass, resembles Graziella in her beauty and naïveté. Her family is the humble circle previously seen in *Graziella,* the *Tailleur de pierres de Saint-Point,* and *Geneviève.* There is compassion shown for the victims of injustice, especially for those wrongly imprisoned. The threadbare plot is nothing but a bundle of Romantic clichés. By presenting the novel as a series of narratives related to the author by Fior and her family, Lamartine only succeeds in making it a rambling and disjointed recitation of events.

XXIII   Mémoires politiques

The *Mémoires politiques* was published in Paris by Lamartine in 1860-66 as volumes XXXVII to XL of a collection of his works.

The *Mémoires politiques* repeats what has been said before. Lamartine recalls the last days of Napoleon, tells about the start of his literary career, and relates his political fortunes up to 1848 with the usual defense of his policies.

Only the specialist who traces down every last detail would find anything of interest in the *Mémoires politiques*. The work is just another in a series of swan songs by a crestfallen politician unreconciled to defeat.

XXIV   Antoniella

Antoniella, a novel, was published in Paris by Michel-Lévy in 1867.

Antoniella, who tells her story to Lamartine, is left penniless by her father's death and seeks refuge with an old friend, Annunziata. The latter's husband dies, and the two young women are unable to care for the children. Antoniella has herself and Annunziata imprisoned on false charges of murder so that the children will be sheltered by the state. Lorenzo, Antoniella's lover, rescues her from prison. In their attempt to escape Lorenzo and Antoniella experience a series of hair-raising adventures. At the end everyone is pardoned, and the children are reunited with Annunziata.

Like Geneviève, Antoniella confesses to a fictitious crime in the hope of sparing undue suffering to loved ones. The claptrap of Lorenzo's flight with Antoniella recalls the escapades of Fior d'Aliza and is a sure sign of Lamartine's senility. *Antoniella* merely proves once more that the bare essentials of novelistic technique were beyond Lamartine. Only when composing history does he have any sense of characterization and movement. Confronted with the task of writing a piece of fiction, he resorts to the most outlandish devices to construct a narrative and plot. There is some merit to the first part of the book where arbitrary arrest and summary trial of social outcasts are touchingly described. The pat ending does not conceal Lamartine's distress over society's unwillingness to alleviate the sufferings of the disadvantaged.

XXV   Memoires inédits

The *Memoires inédits* was published in Paris by Hachette in 1870.

The ancestry of Lamartine's father and grandfather is outlined. There are further details on his early school days. The liaison with Graziella, service under Louis XVIII, and the poet's acquaintance with Joseph de Maistre are all recounted. The *Memoires inédits* furnishes some useful data. More is learned about Graziella and school days at Belley. Of special interest is the description of Guichard de Bienassis' library where Lamartine probably for the first time had access to the writings of Saint-Martin and may even have read in snatches the Marquis de Sade.

XXVI   Manuscrit de ma mère

The *Manuscrit de ma mère*, published in 1871 by Hachette, covered the period from 1801 to 1829 and consisted of excerpts from the journals of Madame de Lamartine and comments by the poet.

Excerpts from the *Confidences* provide much of the background material. The journals record Madame de Lamartine's love of family and religious nature. A fervent reader of the Bible, she helped the poor without public display. She instilled a love of religion in Alphonse, watched him grow up through the Napoleonic Wars, and saw his emergence as a poet. While she disapproved of her son's choice of books by tossing those she judged immoral like *Emile* and *La Nouvelle Héloïse* into the fire, she heartily approved of his selection of Marianne Birch as his bride. After her son's marriage she continued to watch his activities with interest and was alarmed by irreverent passages in the *Dernier Chant*. Just before an unfortunate accident that took her life, she was already resigned to death.

The temptation exists to inquire whether the maternal reminiscences were not a product of Lamartine's own pen. In style and outlook they are a direct reflection of the poet's unique manner of observing and describing past events. All the coloring and wistful sentiment are there. Lamartine may have selected those passages that created the desired impression on readers. The very naïveté of the work is reliable evidence of the atmosphere of praise and adulation in which the poet was reared. Even the rude world of politics never completely dispelled the illusion of grandeur created by those early days.

XXVII   Les Visions

Les Visions, a series of poems originally intended as part of
a long epic, was written between 1823 and 1829. Isolated poems
from *Les Visions* appeared in the *Harmonies* in 1830 and in 1851
other portions of the projected epic were published at the end of
the *Nouvelles Confidences*. *Les Visions* was published in more
complete form in the *Poésies inédites* of 1873, and in 1936 a full
text with commentary was produced by Henri Guillemin.

After a long invocation by the poet in a psalmic mood the
First Vision takes an apocalyptic view of civilization and man's
early history. In the Second Vision Eloïm, a prophet, wanders
about warning people of the Final Judgment. The last section,
"Les Chevaliers," tells the story of Tristan and Hermine killed
by the latter's father, Béranger, who suspected them of dishonor-
ing his name.

"Les Chevaliers" is of little consequence. The character of
Eloïm, however, deserves some attention since his utterances
reflect notions current in France during the 1820's at the time of
the composition of *Les Visions*. The Swedenborgians believed
in an impending Last Judgment and felt the second coming of
Christ was not far off. Eloïm, who was to appear at various
stages of man's development in Lamartine's epic, tells an old
couple the day is near when the Lord will come to judge
mankind:

Eloïm continued: Ah, if you adore Him, by His days and death
sacred to every Christian, by this day that approaches, on which
from the top of the clouds, He will come to awaken and to judge all
the ages, open for a minute this asylum to me![9]

If Lamartine, as has already been observed, did take passing
notice of Swedenborgian thought, he was only sharing an interest
of many contemporaries. Theosophy, in general, was in vogue
during the Romantic period, and Lamartine was attracted to
Saint-Martin. Aside from the theosophic aspects of *Les Visions*,
the poems disclose the broad historical scope of the original
design of Lamartine's epic. *Jocelyn* and *La Chute d'un ange*
were to have been chapters of a longer work. While it was never

completed, Lamartine's attempt at epic poetry placed him with
Hugo as one of the poets who made a noteworthy effort in that
genre in the nineteenth century.

XXVIII Correspondance de Lamartine

The *Correspondance de Lamartine* for the years 1807 to 1852
was edited by Valentine and published posthumously in 1873-74
in six volumes by Hachette. Four years had elapsed since the
poet's death, and the time was appropriate to revive his
reputation.

Most of the correspondence up to 1820 consists of letters
written to two close friends, Aymon de Virieu and Guichard
de Bienassis. In his letters Lamartine refers to his favorite
authors, thoughts on religion and philosophy, and life at school
and at home. Rousseau and Ossian struck his fancy and he
enjoyed the leading writers of seventeenth- and eighteenth-
century France. In translation he read Pope, Shakespeare, Gray,
and Goethe's *Werther* over whom he shed as many tears as he
did over Chateaubriand's *René*.

After 1813 Madame de Staël's *De l'Allemagne* awakened an
interest in philosophy. He now dreamed of putting *Atala* into
verse and planned a playwright's career. The latter ambition
faded with Talma's rejection of *Saül*. With the success of the
Méditations, he emerged as an important poet and shortly afterward married Marianne Birch.

The correspondence of the 1820's relates the details of his
diplomatic service in Italy and continued literary activity. With
the 1830's and the passing of Bourbon influence, Lamartine
feared a revolution and spoke of social progress. He felt the time
was ripe for Catholicism to become more modern and tolerant.
Saddened by his daughter's death in the Near East, he plunged
into politics to overcome his grief. Letters reveal how much he
relished parliamentary debate while at the time producing
further literary works like *Jocelyn* and *La Chute d'un ange.*

During the 1840's the correspondence shows clearly the extent
of the poet-politician's confidence in his own mission. Sensing a
revolution in the making, he wrote the *Histoire des Girondins* to

warn the public against the evils of violent change. Letters for 1848 are scarce, and there is scant reference to the events of that year. The correspondence ends abruptly in 1852 with no indication of the poet's future plans.

Valentine obviously either omitted some letters or did not have them in her possession. She may have wished to conceal evidence of a passionate love life. Even then, the letters reveal a mercurial individual declaring himself at one moment a poet and a politician the next. Much of it may seem sentimental gabble, but he was not the only Romantic to express his feelings freely. After all, he was a direct product of Rousseau and Chateaubriand. Many details in the letters reflect the spirit of Lamartine's poetry and his attitude toward religion. As in the *Harmonies*, he favors an updated Christianity.

One question not answered by the correspondence is whether he intended to put politics before poetry. On one occasion he describes how he defeated the antipoets in the Chamber. Perhaps Lamartine was consciously or unconsciously a poet at all times who attempted to poetize politics. This would account for many an enigmatic speech. A poet who attributed his talent to divine origins would see no contradiction in becoming a visionary with insights denied to ordinary men. Such an interpretation may seem fanciful but does serve to explain Lamartine's tendency to pontificate on all matters.

XXIX *Additional Correspondence*

Letters written by Lamartine and not published in the Valentine edition provide additional information. There are details on romances with Graziella, Julie Charles, Nina Pierreclos, Henriette Pommier, and Lena de Larche. One letter of 1833 has an especially interesting reference to Louis-Claude de Saint-Martin and points to Lamartine's attraction to theosophy.[10] After 1852 the correspondence constitutes a pathetic narrative of the poet's financial plight. The *Cours familier* had a modest sale, but nonetheless creditors hounded him constantly. There is an ambiguous allusion to religious fanaticism that some critics label an anti-Catholic diatribe. This matter will be more fully discussed at the close of this chapter.[11]

XXX *Final State of Lamartine's Religious Views*

The *Poésies inédites,* published in 1871 with Hachette by Valentine, contains little of significance except for one poem "A la croix," with its admission to Christ of the poet's unworthiness:

> I was a man, an ephemeral insect, formed from weakness and pride, a sinner from the womb of my mother and trembling right up to the coffin, between light and doubt, losing and rediscovering my way, faithful yesterday, weak today, like the disciple ashamed to admit to the praetorian he believed in his master. . . .[12]

Throughout "A la croix" the plaintive note of a repentant old man predominates. Since Valentine appended no date to the poem, some have assigned it to an earlier period despite internal evidence it was written by the poet in his declining years. "A la croix" has much the same spirit of resignation as "La Vigne et la maison." Toward the end of his life, Lamartine clung stubbornly to belief in a personal God. He could not stand Jean-Marie Dargaud's agnosticism and disapproved of the affable rationalist's desire to be buried without religious ceremony. Understandably Lamartine's reaction in 1861 to Dargaud's *Histoire de la liberté religieuse et de ses fondateurs* was lukewarm. Hence he wrote to the author: "I have reread recently a part of the book; the stylistic talent is great. Only the subject is repugnant to me. The fanatics of a half-lie are as atrocious as the fanatics of a complete lie. . . ."[13]

Guillemin contends the "fanatics of a complete lie" are the Catholics, but comments in the *Cours familier* clearly show the poet disagreed with Dargaud's thesis that during the Reformation exponents of Catholicism proved themselves more bigoted than those of Protestantism.[14] What Lamartine really opposed was fanatics of any type whether they supported a "half-lie" or a "complete lie." He was no more anti-Catholic in this instance than in 1868 in an article on Voltaire in the *Cours familier,* a tribute to the redoubtable philosopher as a stimulating thinker and writer but not as a theologian. The article in question must have been written several years before, since by 1867 Lamartine was too weak to hold a pen.[15]

His final moments on February 25, 1869 are recorded by Valentine: "I saw only him; he had always told me he wanted to die in the religion of his mother. I don't know whether he was orthodox, or rather, I wish many orthodox persons a heart and a soul as religious as his, praying constantly, and having himself read by me psalms and the *Imitation of Christ....*"[16] Convinced of the sincerity of her uncle's reconciliation with the Church, Valentine only questioned his familiarity with Catholic doctrine. Her implied wish that he could have died with a fuller understanding of Catholicism is far removed from serious misgivings about his faith. Valentine's report of Lamartine's death in no way conflicts with the attitude reflected in his last writings. He became reattached to the sentimental brand of Catholicism espoused in the *Méditations*. This belief represented to him the most personally satisfying approach to God, but unquestionably he would have told other believers to choose their own route. After the rejection of human theologies in "Le Désert" the two poems "La Vigne et la maison" and "À la croix" marked an increasing reliance on Providence. An opponent of intolerance, he sought in religion an ideal divorced from the often disagreeable context of its erroneous application by weak mortals.

CHAPTER 5

Lamartine's Reputation
in France and Abroad

I *French Reaction*

S AINTE-BEUVE explained Lamartine's popularity in the early
days of Romanticism by the manner in which the *Méditations*
rejuvenated French poetry; the critic credited him with a lasting
contribution even though the *Méditations* subsequently became
outmoded. Hugo compared Lamartine to Racine and Musset
admitted the extent of his debt to the author of the *Harmonies.*
Disapproval of Lamartine's politics did not keep Vigny from
admiring his colleague's poetry.

While understandably fellow Romantics in general complimented Lamartine, a succeeding generation, the Parnassians,
scored his excessive sentimentality. Influenced undoubtedly by
this view, Baudelaire and Verlaine joined in the ridicule of
Lamartine. Rimbaud, however, saw in him a visionary hampered
by the old prosody, and Jammes pointed out to Mallarmé his
own indebtedness to Lamartine. While the leader of Symbolism
was affected by the *Méditations,* in Naturalist quarters Zola and
Maupassant heard nothing but scornful references to Lamartine
in the parlors of the Goncourts.

In the twentieth century the debate on Lamartine continued.
Claudel felt he was too bourgeois and debased the spirit of
poetry. Valéry during his lifetime was frequently compared to
Lamartine as an exponent of pure poetry and had the same
concept of the poet's melancholy destiny. Among novelists, Proust
on the whole enjoyed the *Méditations* although he was convinced that Lamartine often failed to give an exact impression
of nature. Despite an ingrained preference for Classicism, Gide
felt the Romantic Lamartine had his place and imparted
harmony and rhythm to the lyric.

108

Thus, the nature of Lamartine's contribution is still a subject of much discussion. Historically his role in Romanticism can not be challenged. The modern epic poem in France can have no adequate treatment without a consideration of *Jocelyn.* In suggesting unconsciously the phonetic value of words without regard to precise meaning he showed new possibilities exploited handily by Parnassian and Symbolist poets. Whether the succeeding generations of writers approved of Lamartine or not, many did read him. It is not too wild a conjecture, perhaps, to see in Flaubert's *Madame Bovary* an occasional passage reminiscent of *Graziella* even though the author was outspoken in his denunciation of Lamartine.

II *European Reaction*

Outside France Lamartine was widely read in Europe in the Romantic period. He was on close terms with Manzoni. The Russian poets, Lermontov and Pushkin, were acquainted with his work, and the Spaniard, Gustavo Becquer in the *Rimas,* betrayed the influence of the *Méditations.* Lamartine also enjoyed considerable favor with English readers during his lifetime. Although considered a Catholic poet, he was welcomed with relief in England by Protestants who, weary of the antireligious cynicism of the Enlightenment, had already seen in Chateaubriand a champion of the consolations of Christianity and spiritual rebirth through faith. Lamartine quickly won supporters among a public in England fond of Chateaubriand; in the *Méditations* they read a similar message of personal communication with God amidst the beauties of nature. Previously scornful of the alleged stiltedness of French verse, British readers readily admitted the *Méditations* was a refreshing exception. Byron could fulminate against Lamartine's effrontery in preaching to him about irreligion in "L'Immortalité" and Thomas Moore might write a caustic parody of "Le Désespoir," but the average informed reader in England had a high opinion of Lamartine. In fashionable circles the French poet enjoyed a substantial reputation. Many wished Lamartine would convert to Protestantism, especially after reading the *Voyage en orient,* available in English shortly after its publication; in the account of his trip to the Holy Land they saw evidence of an acceptance of Christ as a personal saviour. Although contrary to the facts, such an interpretation strengthened Lamartine's reputation in England as a religious poet.

III   *American Reaction*

For much the same reasons Lamartine had a similar success in America.[1] The first information concerning him in the 1820's in the United States was obtained largely through English periodicals. An early disciple of French Romanticism and an admirer of both Chateaubriand and Lamartine, Timothy Flint urged his countrymen to read the *Méditations*. In the poetry of Lamartine Flint saw a potential source of inspiration to American writers dissatisfied with the prevailing subservience to English letters. During the 1830's Lamartine acquired a wider readership, for the *Voyage en orient* was available in English soon after its publication. American critics in the better literary journals analyzed *Jocelyn*, the *Harmonies*, and *La Chute d'un ange*. The eccentric poet of the Transcendentalists, Jones Very, discerned a mystical and epic quality in Lamartine. In an era when most French books were judged too risqué for feminine eyes, he was one of the few writers of France on the reading list at fashionable academies for genteel young ladies in America.

During the 1840's Americans watched with increasing interest Lamartine's literary and political career. The *Voyage en orient* continued to be popular, and the *History of the Girondists* was received with enthusiasm especially by liberals who applauded Lamartine's progressive program for social reform. Whittier, who translated poems from the *Harmonies*, headed the abolitionists jubilant at the prospect of a staunch opponent of slavery becoming leader of the provisional government in 1848. The historian George Bancroft was a close friend of Lamartine and a witness to the exciting days following the abdication of Louis-Philippe. Emerson felt it necessary to watch Lamartine in action in the Chamber of Deputies. Ticknor and other distinguished Americans visited Lamartine when abroad. Understandably in an era of poor communications when inadequate reports traveled slowly, Americans could not comprehend at first why French voters rejected Lamartine. To many in the United States he was the George Washington of France. Brook Farm was typical of a community of American intellectuals shocked by his downfall. Lowell scored the ingratitude of the French and dedicated a poem to the vanquished poet-statesman. In various parts of the United States villages and streets were named after him.

With the 1850's Americans began to understand the reasons why Frenchmen turned against Lamartine. *Raphaël* was a favorite with the ladies, but serious critics were now taking a second look at his works. The exaggerated sentimentality of the *Confidences* and *Graziella* became an object of ridicule. The *Cours familier de littérature,* which Lamartine expected Americans to support in large numbers, attracted few subscribers. A blundering agent sent to America by Lamartine interrupted Longfellow at dinnertime and characterized the ineptitude of the sales campaign. One editor told Lamartine the price alone of the *Cours familier* was exorbitant—without considering the dullness of its contents. Lowell turned against the French poet and now denounced his egoism and opportunism. Infuriated by this cold rejection, Lamartine bitterly attacked American philistinism. When an American poetess interviewed him in France in 1861, Lamartine scoffed at her suggestion that he lecture in New York where, he insisted, he would only be the object of idle curiosity. Abandoning his previous stand on abolition, Lamartine supported the South in the Civil War and proclaimed slavery a satisfactory institution for black people. Napoleon III's invasion of Mexico was to him an excellent opportunity to bring French culture to benighted Mexicans. American observers good-naturedly shrugged their shoulders and attributed Lamartine's outbursts to the frustrations of old age. After his death there were those who remembered America's first contact with the *Méditations* whose message had some meaning for a Protestant society caught up in the revivalistic spirit of the Second Great Awakening. Just as France later reassessed the contributions of Lamartine, so did Americans have fond memories of the plaintive strains of the *Méditations* and *Harmonies.*

Conclusion

Lamartine will always be remembered at the very least as the poet who revitalized lyric poetry in France. He was rather modern in his subjective slant on nature, mankind, and religion. Affected somewhat by the theosophy of Saint-Martin, he assumed a sacerdotal role in revealing metaphysical truths to readers and a hieratic tone in political speeches that confounded and irritated opponents. His Eclecticism consisted of various and conflicting components scattered through his writings, and he was probably the first French poet to take an interest in Hinduism. From the religious sentimentalism of his first poems he went on to treat social themes and then returned to a personalist approach to the deity in "La Vigne et la maison" after the ideological catharsis of "Le Désert." Not always effete or melancholic, he could on occasion express a vigorous love of his native soil. While seldom associated with the Parnassians or Symbolists, he did have an eye for plastic beauty and an ear for the subtle musical effects of felicitous word combinations.

As prosateur, Lamartine usually receives less attention although a prolific writer of prose. His best single work is the *Histoire des Girondins*, noteworthy for its well-paced narrative and its striking character sketches. To a lesser degree the *Histoire des Constituants* has many of the same merits. Despite its unevenness, the *Cours familier de littérature* is a valuable record of Lamartine's views on contemporaries and literature in general. Granted the sensitivity to, and awareness of, social injustice reflected in their pages his attempts at novel-writing only indicate his outdated and simplistic notions of novelistic technique.

In the theater Lamartine fared little better. Talma's refusal to appear in *Saül* discouraged him for over thirty years until finally the dismal record of *Toussaint L'Ouverture* convinced him to abandon the theater. Attracted by facets of the Romantic drama, he still remained Classical in taste. Much of Shakespeare he found unpalatable, preferring instead the scintillating comedy of Molière and the polished Racinian line.

A propitious time and occasion enabled Lamartine to realize the dream of many Romantics in actually becoming a leader of his people. The dream soon faded, but he left the memory of an honest effort to maintain peace in Europe. Today, in retrospect Lamartine's record is far more creditable than that of other political figures faced with the same problems.

In the preface it was stated that Lamartine did not deserve

the neglect his opponents might wish. With all his shortcomings, he still cannot be callously written off in any serious study of French literature and history. Without him the picture of Romanticism is incomplete and an understanding of subsequent developments in French poetry is inadequate. Lamartine may yet see the day when his place in the literature of France is defined and established beyond question.

Notes and References

Chapter One

1. Readers are referred to H. R. Whitehouse, *Life of Lamartine* (Boston: Houghton Mifflin, 1918), 2 vols., and M. Toesca, *Lamartine, ou l'amour de la vie* (Paris: Albin Michel, 1969), for details on the poet's life.

2. A useful reference on the political situation in 1848 is Paul H. Beik, *Louis Philippe and the July Monarchy* (Princeton: Nostrand, 1965).

3. Lamartine had access to J. D. Guigniaut's *Religions de l'antiquité* (Paris: Treuttel, 1825), a translation of Friedrich Creuzer's *Symbolik und Mythologie der alten Völker.* Raymond Schwab, *La renaissance orientale* (Paris: Payot, 1950), discusses the furore created by Guigniaut-Creuzer in literary circles.

4. Sainte-Beuve first remarked the Martinist tone in Lamartine, *Portraits contemporains* (Paris: Didier, 1847), I, 199-200. For ideas and imagery Lamartine borrowed from Louis-Claude de Saint-Martin see *Le Ministère de l'homme-esprit* (Paris: Migneret, 1802), p. 35, and *Tableau naturel des rapports qui existent entre Dieu, l'homme et la nature* (Edinburgh: 1782), II, 127-30. See also Robert Amadou, *Louis-Claude de Saint-Martin et le martinisme* (Paris: Editions du Griffon d'or, 1946).

5. For a discussion of this point see my thesis "A Reevaluation of Lamartine's Eclecticism," unpublished doctoral dissertation at the University of Wisconsin, 1953.

Chapter Two

1. The most complete collection of Lamartine's poetry is the *Oeuvres poétiques complètes,* edited by Marius-François Guyard and published by Gallimard in the *Bibliothèque de la Pléiade* (Paris, 1963). References to Lamartine's poems unless otherwise indicated are to the Guyard edition identified simply by page numbers.

2. P. 3. All translations are my own.

> Cependant, s'élancant de la flèche gothique,
> Un son religieux se répand dans les airs,

Le voyageur s'arrête, et la cloche rustique
Aux derniers bruits du jour mêle de saints concerts.

3. P. 6.

Borné dans sa nature, infini dans ses voeux,
L'homme est un dieu tombé qui se souvient des cieux. . . .

4. P. 13.

Le soir ramène le silence.
Assis sur ces rochers déserts,
Je suis dans le vague des airs
Le char de la nuit qui s'avance.

5. P. 18.

Après un vain soupir, après l'adieu suprême
De tout ce qui t'aimait, n'est-il plus rien qui t'aime?
Ah! sur ce grand secret n'interroge que toi!
Vois mourir ce qui t'aime, Elvire, et réponds-moi!

6. P. 24.

Héritiers des douleurs, victimes de la vie,
Non, non, n'espérez pas que sa rage assouvie
        Endorme le Malheur!
Jusque'à ce que la Mort, ouvrant son aile immense,
Engloutisse à jamais dans l'éternel silence
        L'éternelle douleur!

7. P. 24.

Quoi! le fils du néant a maudit l'existence!
Quoi! tu peux m'accuser de mes propres bienfaits!
Tu peux fermer tes yeux à la magnificence
        Des dons que je t'ai faits!

8. P. 36.

La gloire est le rêve d'une ombre;
Elle a trop retranché le nombre
Des jours qu'elle devait charmer.
Tu veux que je lui sacrifie
Ce dernier souffle de ma vie!
Je veux le garder pour aimer.

9. P. 39.

Eternité, néant, passé, sombres abîmes,
Que faites-vous des jours que vous engloutissez?
Parlez: nous rendrez-vous ces extases sublimes
        Que vous nous ravissez?

10. For Saint-Martin's description paraphrased by Lamartine see
Tableau naturel, II, 127.

P. 46.
Voilà le sacrifice immense, universel!
L'univers est le temple, et la terre est l'autel;
Les cieux en sont le dôme: et ces astres sans nombre,
Ces feux demi-voilés, pâle ornement de l'ombre,
Dans la voûte d'azur avec ordre semés,
Sont les sacrés flambeaux pour ce temple allumés. . . .

11. P. 46.
Ame de l'univers, Dieu, père, créateur,
Sous tous ces noms divers je crois en toi, Seigneur. . . .

12. P. 53.
Cette raison superbe, insuffisant flambeau,
S'éteint comme la vie aux portes du tombeau. . . .

13. P. 64.
Dieu! que les airs sont doux! Que la lumière est pure!
Tu règnes en vainqueur sur toute la nature. . . .

14. P. 69.
Tous ces fronts prosternés, ce feu qui les embrase,
Ces parfums, ces soupirs s'exhalant du saint lieu,
Ces élans enflammés, ces larmes de l'extase,
Tout me répond que c'est un Dieu.

15. P. 71.
Terre, soleil, vallons, belle et douce nature,
Je vous dois une larme aux bords de mon tombeau,
L'air est si parfumé! la lumière est si pure!
Aux regards d'un mourant le soleil est si beau!

16. P. 83.
Silence, ô lyre, et vous silence,
Prophètes, voix de l'avenir!
Tout l'univers se tait d'avance
Devant celui qui doit venir!

17. P. 123.
Son cercueil est fermé! Dieu l'a jugé. Silence!
Son crime et ses exploits pèsent dans la balance!
Que des faibles mortels la main n'y touche plus!
Qui peut sonder, Seigneur, ta clémence infinie?
Et vous, fléaux de Dieu, qui sait si le génie
            N'est pas une de vos vertus?

18. P. 171.
Quand le peuple est tyran, ils insultent aux rois.

19. P. 128.
S'enivrer de parfums, de lumière et d'azur;
Secouant, jeune encor, la poudre de ses ailes,

    S'envoler comme un souffle aux voûtes éternelles,
    Voilà du papillon le destin enchanté!
20. P. 141.
    De l'amandier tige fleurie,
    Symbole, hélas, de la beauté,
    Comme toi, la fleur de la vie
    Fleurit et tombe avant l'été.
21. P. 145.
    Le poète est semblable aux oiseaux de passage,
    Qui ne bâtissent point leurs nids sur le rivage,
    Qui ne se posent point sur les rameaux des bois;
    Nonchalamment bercés sur le courant de l'onde,
    Ils passent en chantant loin des bords, et le monde
        Ne connaît rien d'eux, que leur voix.
22. P. 164.
    Oui, je reviens à toi, berceau de mon enfance,
    Embrasser pour jamais tes foyers protecteurs.
    Loin de moi les cités et leur vaine opulence!
        Je suis né parmi les pasteurs!
23. P. 174.
    Les saints flambeaux jetaient une dernière flamme,
    Le prêtre murmurait ces doux chants de la mort,
    Pareils aux chants plaintifs que murmure une femme
        A l'enfant qui s'endort.
24. P. 105.
    Encore un peu de temps, et votre auguste foule,
    Roulant avec l'erreur de l'olympe qui croule,
    Fera place au Dieu, saint, unique, universel,
    Le seul Dieu que j'adore et qui n'a point d'autel.
25. P. 199.
    Cherchant ces grands esprits qu'elle a jadis aimés,
    De soleil en soleil, de système en système,
    Elle vole et se perd avec l'âme qu'elle aime,
    De l'espace infini suit les vastes détours,
    Et dans le sein de Dieu se retrouve toujours!
26. P. 92.
    La vie est le combat, la mort est la victoire,
    Et la terre est pour nous l'autel expiatoire. . . .
27. P. 267.
    Mais les temps ne sont plus! le passé les emporte:
    Le ciel parle à la terre une langue plus forte;
    C'est la seule raison qui l'explique à la foi!
    Les grands événements, voilà les grands prestiges!

28. P. 205.
   Jupiter, Mahomet, héros, grands hommes, dieux,
   O Christ, pardonne-lui, ne sont rien à ses yeux. . . .
29. P. 205.
   Le Dieu qu'adore Harold est cet agent suprême
   Ce Pan mystérieux, insoluble problème
   Grand, borné, bon, mauvais, que ce vaste univers
   Révèle à ses regards sous mille aspects divers.
   Etre sans attributs, force sans providence,
   Exerçant au hasard une aveugle puissance. . . .
30. P. 291.
   Mais c'est surtout ton nom, ô roi de la nature,
   Qui fait vibrer en moi cet instrument divin;
   Quand j'invoque ce nom, mon coeur plein de murmure
   Résonne comme un temple où l'on chante sans fin.
31. P. 304.
   Reportez dans les cieux, l'hommage de l'aurore,
   Montez, il est là-haut, descendez, tout est lui!
32. P. 313.
   A défaut des clartés, il nous compte un désir.
   La voix qui crie Allah! la voix qui dit mon Père,
   Lui portent l'encens pur et l'encens adultère:
   A lui seul de choisir.
33. P. 365.
   D'un passé sans mémoire incertaines reliques,
   Mystères d'un vieux monde en mystères écrits!
   Et vous, temples debout, superbes basiliques,
   Dont un souffle divin anime les parvis!
34. P. 478.
   Voilà la vérité! Chaque siècle à son tour
   Croit soulever son voile et marcher à son jour,
   Mais celle qu'aujourd'hui notre ignorance adore
   Demain n'est qu'un nuage; une autre est près d'éclore!
35. P. 428.
   J'ai cherché le Dieu que j'adore,
   Partout où l'instinct m'a conduit. . . .
36. P. 415.
   Pour moi, soit que ton nom ressuscite ou succombe,
   O Dieu de mon berceau sois le Dieu de ma tombe!
37. P. 399.
   Creusez-moi dans ces champs la couche que j'envie
   Et ce dernier sillon où germe une autre vie.

38. P. 335.
   Voilà l'errante hirondelle
   Qui rase du bout de l'aile
   L'eau dormante des marais.
   Voilà l'enfant des chaumières
   Qui glane sur les bruyères
   Le bois tombé des forêts.
39. P. 457.
   Oh! mêle ta voix à la mienne!
   La même oreille nous entend;
   Mais ta prière aérienne
   Monte mieux au ciel qui l'attend!
40. P. 351.
   Et j'entends bourdonner sous l'herbe que je foule
   Ces flots d'êtres vivants que chaque sillon roule:
   Atomes animés par le souffle divin,
   Chaque rayon du jour en élève sans fin. . . .
41. P. 516. "Les Révolutions" appeared in an 1832 edition o
the *Harmonies*.
   Marchez! l'humanité ne vit pas d'une idée!
   Elle éteint chaque soir celle qui l'a guidée,
   Elle en allume une autre à l'immortel flambeau:
   Comme ces morts vêtus de leur parure immonde,
   Les générations emportent de ce monde
           Leurs vêtements dans le tombeau!
42. P. 517.
   Sous le vôtre! o Chrétiens! l'homme en qui Dieu travaille
   Change éternellement de formes et de taille. . . .
43. P. 386.
   Loi sainte et mystérieuse!
   Une âme mélodieuse
   Anime tout l'univers;
   Chaque être a son harmonie,
   Chaque étoile son génie,
   Chaque élément ses concerts.
44. P. 464.
   Mais le sens qui t'adore a grandi dans mon âme,
   C'est le seul désormais dont ma vie ait besoin,
   Il voit, il sent, il touche, il entend, il proclame
   Les choses de plus haut et son Dieu de plus loin!
45. P. 459.
   C'était ce grand esprit, cette âme universelle,
   Qui vivait, qui sentait, qui végétait, pour elle;

Etre presque divin dont elle était le corps,
Qui de sa masse inerte agitait les ressorts. . . .

46. In Guigniaut's translation of Creuzer, *Religions de l'Antiquité*, is the following pantheistic passage on p. 275:

La grande âme . . . se confond avec Dieu Lui-même . . . c'est la grande âme qui fait vivre tous les êtres et vit elle-même en eux. . . .

47. For Saint-Martin's reference to man as the book of God, see *Ministère de l'Homme-Esprit*, p. 195.

P. 375.

Du grand livre de la nature,
Si la lettre, à vos yeux obscure,
Ne le trahit pas en tout lieu.
Ah! l'homme est le livre suprême:
Dans les fibres de son coeur même
Lisez, mortels: Il est un Dieu!

48. P. 372.

Autour du cou blanc qu'elle embrasse,
Comme un collier elle s'enlace,
Descend, serpente, il vient rouler
Sur un sein où s'enflent à peine
Deux sources d'où la vie humaine
En ruisseaux d'amour doit couler!

Chapter Three

1. Henri Guillemin, *Connaissance de Lamartine* (Fribourg: Librairie de l'Université, 1942), p. 165.

As-tu donc oublié que si la main du brave
Sent battre encor un coeur dans l'Italie esclave
C'est que l'ombre de Rome est encore au milieu?

2. For Saint-Martin's reference to man as a priest see *Tableau Naturel*, II, 127-30.

P. 534.

Voilà l'homme, voilà le pontife immortel!
Pontife que Dieu fit pour parfumer l'autel,
Pour dérober au sphinx le mot de la nature,
Pour jeter son flambeau dans notre nuit obscure,
Et nous faire épeler, dans ces divins accents,
Ce grand livre du sort dont lui seul a le sens.

3. *Méditations poétiques*, "Destinées de la poésie," ed. G. Lanson (Paris: Hachette, 1915), II, 413.

La poésie sera de la raison chantée, voilà sa destinée pour longtemps; elle sera philosophique, religieuse, politique, sociale, comme les époques que le genre humain va traverser; elle sera intime surtout, personnelle, meditative, et grave; non plus un jeu de l'esprit, un caprice mélodieux de la pensée légère et superficielle, mais l'écho profond, réel, sincère, des plus hautes conceptions de l'intelligence, des plus mystérieuses impressions de l'âme. . . .

4. *Souvenirs, impressions, pensées, et paysages pendant un voyage en orient* (Paris: Pagnerre, 1854), I, 171. Stanhope calls the poet "un de ces hommes de désir."

5. P. 641.

Ah! s'il en est, doux souffles de l'aurore,
Emportez-nous avec l'encens des fleurs,
Emportez-nous où les âmes sont soeurs!
Nous prierons mieux le Dieu que l'astre adore. . . .

6. P. 678.

Vous n'êtes plus Chrétien ni prêtre de Jésus:
Retirez-vous de moi . . . je ne vous connais plus!

7. P. 756.

Je ne surcharge pas leur sens et leur esprit
Du stérile savoir dont l'orgueil se nourrit;
Bien plus que leur raison j'instruis leur conscience:
La nature et leurs yeux, c'est toute ma science!

8. P. 758. (See note 46 of preceding chapter on Hinduism in Lamartine.)

C'est donc cette âme immense, infinie, immortelle,
Qui voit plus que l'étoile, et qui vivra plus qu'elle!

9. P. 686.

O Christ, j'ai comme toi sué mon agonie
Dans ces trois doubles nuits d'horreur et d'insomnie!

10. P. 753.

Quand ces pêcheurs, quittant la barque évangélique,
Tendaient sur l'univers leur filet politique. . . .

11. P. 744.

La terre, qui se fend sous le soc qu'elle aiguise,
En tronçons palpitants s'amoncelle et se brise;
Et, tout en s'entr'ouvrant, fume comme une chair
Qui se fend et palpite et fume sous le fer.

12. P. 926.

O Père, disait-il, de toute créature,
Dont le temple est partout où s'étend la nature,

Dont la présence creuse et comble l'infini,
Que ton nom soit partout dans toute âme béni!
13. Pp. 827-28.
Ses cheveux, qu'agitait le vent léger du soir,
Ondoyaient sur ses bras comme un grand voile noir,
Laissant briller dehors ou ses épaules blanches,
Ou la rondeur du sein, ou les contours des hanches. . . .
14. P. 965.
Un navire céleste à l'étrange figure,
Couvrant un pan des airs de sa vaste envergure. . . .
15. P. 942. (See Note 4 in Chapter 1 on Martinism.)
Le seul divin livre dans lequel il écrit
Son nom toujours croissant, homme, c'est ton esprit!
C'est ta raison, miroir de la raison suprême,
Où se peint dans ta nuit quelque ombre de lui-même.
16. P. 946.
Où le tout est partie et la partie entière;
Où la vie et la mort, le temps et la matière,
Ne sont rien en effet que formes de l'esprit,
Cercles mystérieux que tout en lui décrit. . . .
17. P. 955.
Le code social à grandir destiné,
A dans notre nature un fondement inné:
Cet ineffable instinct de justice suprême
Qui proteste en secret en nous contre nous-même. . . .
18. P. 1110. (See Note 3 in Chapter 1 on Hinduism.)
Alors dans le grand tout mon âme répandue
A fondu, faible goutte au sein des mers perdue,
Que roule l'Océan, insensible fardeau!
Mais où l'impulsion sereine ou convulsive,
Qui de l'abîme entier de vague en vague arrive,
Palpite dans la goutte d'eau.
19. P. 1153.
Un seule culte enchaîne le monde,
Que vivifie un seul amour:
Son dogme, où la lumière abonde,
N'est qu'un Evangile au grand jour. . . .
20. P. 1153.
C'est le Verbe pur du Calvaire,
Non tel qu'en terrestres accents
L'écho lointain du sanctuaire
En laissa fuir le divin sens. . . .

Chapter Four

1. P. 1480.
   Et par quel mot pour toi veux-tu que je me nomme?
   Et par quel sens veux-tu que j'apparaisse à l'homme?
   Est-ce l'oeil, ou l'oreille, ou la bouche, ou la main?
   Qu'est-il en toi de Dieu? Qu'est-il en moi d'humain?
2. P. 1481.
   Du jour où de l'Éden la clarté s'éteignit,
   L'Antiquité menteuse en songe peignit. . . .
3. P. 1482.
   Où dans l'immensité Dieu même s'évapore,
   D'éléments confondus pêle-mêle brutal
   Où le bien n'est plus bien, où le mal n'est plus mal. . . .
4. P. 1483.
   O Mystère! lui dis-je, eh bien! sois donc ma foi. . . .
   Mystére, ô saint rapport du Créateur à moi!
5. P. 1485.
   Je n'aime des longs jours que l'heure des ténèbres,
   Je n'écoute des chants que ces strophes funèbres,
   Que sanglote le prêtre en menant un cercueil.
6. P. 1485.
   Cette heure a pour nos sens des impressions douces
   Comme des pas muets qui marchent sur des mousses. . . .
7. P. 1493.
   Toi qui fis la mémoire, est-ce pour qu'on oublie?
   Non, c'est pour rendre au temps à la fin tous ses jours,
   Pour faire confluer, là-bas, en un seul cours
   Le passé, l'avenir, ces deux moitiés de vie
   Dont l'une dit jamais et l'autre dit toujours
   Ce passé, doux Éden dont notre âme est sortie,
   De notre éternité ne fait-il pas partie?
8. P. 1493.
   O douce Providence! O mère de famille
   Dont l'immense foyer de tant d'enfants fourmille,
   Et qui les vois pleurer souriante au milieu,
   Souviens-toi, coeur du ciel, que la terre est ta fille
   Et que l'homme est parent de Dieu!

9. *Les Visions,* ed. H. Guillemin (Paris: Société d'Editions Les Belles Lettres, 1936), p. 145.
   Eloïm poursuivit: Ah! si vous l'adorez,
   Par ses jours et sa mort à tout chrétien sacrés,

Par ce jour qui s'approche, où du haut des nuages,
Il viendra réveiller et juger tous les âges,
Ouvrez pour un moment cet asile à mes pas!

10. See Maurice Levaillant's edition of the *Correspondance générale de 1830 à 1848* (Paris: E. Droz, 1943).

11. See Henri Guillemin, *Lettres des années sombres* (Fribourg: Société d'Éditions de la librairie de l'Université, 1943).

12. Pp. 1773-74.

Je fus homme, insecte éphémère,
Pétri de faiblesse et d'orgueil,
Pécheur dès le sein de ma mère
Et chancelant jusqu'au cercueil;
Entre la lumière et le doute
Perdant et retrouvant ma route,
Fidèle hier, faible aujourd'hui,
Comme le disciple au prétoire
A son maître honteux de croire....

13. Henri Guillemin, *Lettres des années sombres* (Fribourg, Société d'Éditions de la librairie de l'Université, 1945), p. 158.

J'ai relu ces jours-ci une partie du livre; le talent de style est grand. Seulement, le sujet m'est antipathique. Les fanatiques d'un demi-mensonge sont aussi atroces que les fanatiques du mensonge tout entier.

In the same period Lamartine also said to Dargaud on the same subject, "Pourquoi malgré tous mes conseils avez-vous consacré aux Protestants ce souffle épique dont vous êtes enivré? Ils n'en sont pas dignes." Jean des Cognets, *La vie intérieure de Lamartine* (Paris: Mercure de France, 1913), p. 30.

14. *Cours familier de littérature*, VII, 102-3. Here Lamartine criticizes Dargaud for not admitting that both Catholics and Protestants were equally guilty of bigotry during the Reformation.

15. *Ibid.*, XXVIII, 256. Lamartine praises Voltaire's tolerance but deplores his lack of religious feeling.

16. Charles Alexandre, *Souvenirs sur Lamartine* (Paris: Charpentier, 1884), p. 393.

Je ne voyais que lui; il m'avait toujours dit qu'il voulait mourir dans la religion de sa mère. Je ne sais pas s'il était orthodoxe, ou plutôt je souhaite à bien des orthodoxes un coeur et une âme aussi religieuse que les siens, priant sans cesse, se faisant lire par moi des psaumes et l'*Imitation*....

Chapter Five

1. See my book *French Romanticism on the Frontier* (Madrid: Gredos, 1972) for a detailed discussion of Lamartine's literary fortunes in America.

Selected Bibliography

Bibliographies

References listed below provide the reader with information on some helpful editions of Lamartine's works, bibliographies, and some useful studies.

Thième, *Bibliographie de la littérature française de 1800 à 1930.* Paris: Droz, 1933.

Talvart et Place, *Bibliographie des auteurs modernes de langue française (1801-1962).* Paris: Editions de la Chronique des lettres françaises, 1928-62.

For recent ṣtudies, quarterly bibliographies of *La Revue d'histoire littéraire de la France* (RHLF) and *La Revue de littérature comparée* (RLC) may be consulted as well as the annual bibliographies of PMLA.

PRIMARY SOURCES

Translations

Graziella. Tr. S. C. Barnes. Philadelphia: Lippincott, 1872.

History of the French Revolution of 1848. Tr. Francis A. Durivage and William S. Chase. Boston: Phillips, Sampson, 1849. 2 v. in 1.

History of the Girondists. Tr. H. T. Ryde. New York: Harper, 1848. 3 vols.

History of the Restoration of Monarchy in France. Tr. Captain Rafter. London: Vizetelly, 1851-1853.

Jocelyn. Tr. Hazel P. Stuart. New York: Exposition Press, 1954.

Pilgrimage to the Holy Land (Voyage en orient). Tr. Anon. London: R. Bentley, 1837.

Poetical Meditations of M. Alphonse de La Martine. Tr. Henry Christmas. London: J. W. Parker, 1839.

Raphaël. Tr. Anon. New York: Harper, 1849.

Translations from the Meditations of Lamartine. Tr. James T. Smith. New York: C. Shephard, 1852.

Editions

ALPHONSE DE LAMARTINE. *Le Civilisateur*. Paris: Chez l'auteur, 1852-
54. 3 vols.
————. *Cours familier de littérature*. Paris: Chez l'auteur, 1856-69.
28 vols.
————. *Oeuvres complètes*. Paris: Chez l'auteur, 1860-63. 40 vols.
This collection comprises the major prose and poetic works of
Lamartine except for others listed here.
————. *Oeuvres poétiques complètes*. Ed. Marius-François Guyard.
Paris: Gallimard, 1963 (Bibliothèque de la Pléïade).

SECONDARY SOURCES

Studies on Lamartine

ALEXANDRE, CHARLES. *Souvenirs sur Lamartine, par son secrétaire
intime*. Paris: Charpentier, 1884. A useful source of information
often overlooked.
CITOLEUX, MARC. *La poésie philosophique au XIXe siècle: Lamartine*.
Paris: Champion, 1906. A comprehensive but dated study.
GEORGE, ALBERT J. *Lamartine and Romantic Unanimism*. New York:
Columbia University Press, 1940. Caution must be exercised in
separating useful data from far-fetched thesis.
GUILLEMIN, HENRI. *Le Jocelyn de Lamartine*. Paris: Boivin, 1935.
A great help to the wary researcher on his guard against Guil-
lemin's snap judgments.
————. *Lamartine, L'homme et l'oeuvre*. Paris: Boivin, 1940. Useful
volume despite Guillemin's frequently dubious conclusions.
IRESON, JOHN C. *Lamartine: A Revaluation*. Hull: University of Hull,
1969. A thoughtful reappraisal of Lamartine in light of contemporary viewpoints.
LACRETELLE, HENRI DE. *Lamartine et ses amis*. Paris: Maurice Drey-
fous, 1878. Old but helpful source of information on Lamartine's
circle of friends.
LUPPÉ, MARQUIS DE. *Les Travaux et les jours d'Alphonse de Lamartine*. Paris: Albin Michel, 1952. Fairly recent and informative
work.
TOESCA, MAURICE. *Lamartine, ou l'amour de la vie*. Paris: Albin
Michel, 1969. Rather comprehensive summary of present state
of knowledge on Lamartine marred by unquestioning acceptance
of Guillemin's conclusions.
WHITEHOUSE, HENRY R. *Life of Lamartine*. Boston: Houghton Mifflin, 1918. 2 vols. An old but still serviceable biography and the
most detailed one in English.

Index